CHRISTIAN SOCIAL MINISTRY

CHRISTIAN SOCIAL MINISTRY

■

AN INTRODUCTION

■

DERREL R. WATKINS

BROADMAN
&HOLMAN
PUBLISHERS

Nashville, Tennessee

© Copyright • 1994 Broadman & Holman Publishers
All Rights Reserved
4210-73
ISBN: 0-8054-1073-2
Dewey Decimal Classification: 259
Subject Headings: CHRISTIAN SOCIAL MINISTRIES
Library of Congress Catalog Number: 93-12388
Printed in the United States of America

Unless otherwise stated, all Scripture quotations are from the Holy Bible, *New International Version*, copyright © 1978 New York International Bible Society. Scripture quotations marked (NASB) are from the *New American Standard Bible*, © The Lockman Foundation, 1960, 1962, 1963, 1968, 1971, 1972, 1973, 1975, 1977.

Library of Congress-in-Publication Data

Watkins, Derrel R., 1935-
  Christian social ministry: an introduction / by Derrel R.
  Watkins
    p. cm.
  Includes bibliographical references.
  ISBN 0-8054-1073-2
  1. Church work.   I. Title
BV4400.W38   1994
253—dc20

                                               93-12388
                                                    CIP

Table of Contents

Foreword vi

Preface ix

Chapter 1—Historical Foundations for
Christian Social Ministry. 1

Chapter 2—Organizational Models for
Christian Social Ministry. 21

Chapter 3—Biblical Foundations for
Christian Social Ministries 45

Chapter 4—Theological Foundations for
Christian Social Ministry. 72

Chapter 5—Philosophical Foundations
for Christian Social Ministry 90

Chapter 6—Methods and Skills for Social
Ministry 114

Chapter 7—Christian Social Minister
Roles 145

Chapter 8—Programming for Social
Ministry 159

Foreword

In *Christian Social Ministry: An Introduction* Derrel Watkins welds together an interesting summation of the historical, foundational, philosophical, methodological and programmatic aspects for a better understanding of Christian social ministries. Although the content is expansive, the material is refreshing in its content and delightful to read in its easy free-flowing context. Very visible in the body of the materials are delightful illustrations and stories of experiences with persons in the practice of Christian social ministry. It is a new approach for a social ministry text and will be an enjoyment to read.

We are all aware that the field of social ministries takes place in churches and synagogues throughout the world. This is nothing new in the world of ministry. Social ministries have been a major part of the cultural climate from the time of the ancients as a part of their religious faith. However, each society and culture has had its social ministry context whether identified with world religions or not. Secular and religious societies could not exist without a conscious plan for social ministry as part of their sociological framework. World rulers have risen or fallen often based on the intentionality of their social reforms systems. Our own nation suffers from a lack of creative consciousness toward social reforms and health care. At the beginning of this text is a carefully laid historical overview of the cultures of world history and their intentionality or lack of concern toward social ministry.

As society progressed and a strong Christian faith developed, Christian social ministry, because of its historical identification in the writings of the Old and New Testaments, developed a premeditated design for the practice of social ministries as an important facet of the Christian Church. This is true of the Reformation as well as the growth of European and American Christianity. Although much of Christian social ministry was relegated to organizations outside the church (i.e. Salvation Army, Volunteers of America, Salvationists, and Rescue Missions), many denominations and churches operated in a Christian social ministry context by design. Denominational models are replete in the histories of expanding denominationalism throughout the world.

Within the growth of Christian social ministries in the denominations, a growing awareness of this caring ministry was recognized and included in early seminary educational curricular designs. Christian social ministry became a practical theological stack pole for much of the practical theology which was being practiced in denominations and churches. Seminary courses became a necessity because of the numerous nonchurch organizations, such as programs organized to care for the elderly. By default, denominations and churches entered into robust programs of social ministries. On many occasions the denominations had to play catch up with the nonchurch organizations which "out *social ministered*" them at every turn of the caring ministry. As theological seminaries recognized the need for instruction in social ministry, their denominations sometimes became interested in social ministry programs.

All social ministry, of course, has its origin in the biblical context of the Word of God. If Christian social ministry is not a part of the teaching of the Bible, of what value is it to the church? However, it is an imperative of both the Old and New Testaments. The Old Testament spoke of righteousness, justice, mercy, and love while the New Testament, through the teachings of Christ and His followers, demonstrated the context of Christian social ministry as the cornerstone of practical Christianity demonstrated in physical circumstances. In fact, one of the first controversies of the newly formed church in Jerusalem was the social ministry problem of caring for the "Grecian *widows*." From biblical time, the church has been vitally interested in Christian social ministries, though not always clearly understanding how these ministries might be put into practical operation. Nevertheless, the church has a mandate to "care *for the poor, widows, and orphans*" and this mandate can be served best through an intentional program of Christian social ministry. This book does an exceptional job of presenting the need for accepting the commandment of the Testaments.

After a convincing historical investigation, Derrel Watkins turns to the study of the necessity of a theological and philosophical framework for Christian social ministry. This framework includes a theological foundation for Christian social ministry which provides a biblical imperative for ministry at a human level of the truths which are theologically implied. This includes the doctrine of God's love for His creation, the doctrine of humanity, and the doctrine of redemption, which leads to the doctrine of caring and helping those who are crushed by the limitations and stresses of human life. God is concerned about His creation and expects us to care in similar fashion.

In the philosophical discussion, emphasis is placed on the necessity of social care to a hurting world. The definition of Christian social ministry is developed, followed by principles and practices which could generate an adequate Christian social ministry program. Additional facets of Christian ministry are introduced, such as evangelism, care facilities, and ministerial positions, which gives credence to the necessity for the Christian social ministers as staff positions in denominations and churches. If Christian social ministry is commanded and needs to be practiced through the denomination and church, then experts trained in the field of Christian social ministry need to be available to fill these church and denominational staff positions.

The final three chapters of the book address the training and skill which Christian social ministers need to perform adequately in Christian social ministry. Couched in psychology and social work practices, intervention strategies, intervention tools, and the skills for social ministry, these subjects need to be learned and practiced by trained practitioners. Roles of the Christian social minister, which have risen to the fore in recent years, provide unparalleled opportunities for individuals who desire to work actively in Christian social ministry settings. Because of a serious need for active Christian social ministry, many of the programming needs have already been established. What is needed are persons to fill the roles and put the programs into practice.

Christian social ministry has needed a book of this sort. The book accomplishes a mammoth task of incorporating and interpolating a vast sea of information about Christian social ministry from the historical past to well-organized ministry which was commanded and emphasized by the writings of the Testaments. Written from a crucible of practice in the church, as a seminary professor and as a practitioner on the streets and in the rescue missions, Derrel Watkins has placed the emphasis of Christian social ministry squarely in our laps with a basic question, *"Here is a needed ministry; what are we going to do about it?"*

It has been a pleasure to write this foreword for my good friend and colleague of many years at Southwestern Baptist Theological Seminary.

Jack D. Terry, Jr.
Dean, School of Religious Education
Southwestern Baptist Theological Seminary
Fort Worth, Texas

Preface

This book is about the historical, biblical, theological, philosophical, and methodological cornerstones upon which effective helping is built. It is also about social ministry as it is implemented as a major function of the church.

The foundational concept of this book is drawn from Leviticus 19:18, as quoted in Matthew 22:39; Mark 12:31; and Luke 10:27. In these passages Jesus provided an enlarged interpretation of the law in emphasizing what a righteous neighbor does when motivated by God-like love. He contrasted this interpretation with the practice of the traditional definition of a neighbor. A godly person reaches out to help any person who is hurting, no matter what group that person belongs to. For Jesus, it was and is more important to love and help any person in need than to segregate the worthy from the unworthy. In fact, according to Jesus, there are no unworthy persons. All ministry is built upon this *agape* love foundation.

Definitions

Let's define our terms as we will use them in this book. The term helping is a synonym for ministry. The verb form of the word *minister*, according to *Webster's New World Dictionary*, means "to serve, give, help, fill wants, or act as an agent for another." In this book we will be using "minister" and "help" interchangeably.

Helping one another in times of need has been a function of societies since the beginning of the human race. Although the help may take different forms, all cultures have formalized ways of aiding persons in need. In most societies when persons are in trouble, the family comes to their aid. Western civilization is unique in that much of aid is expected to come from societal resources administered by governments. Contemporary forms of help from churches stem from a long history of helping persons that is both traditional and commanded by God.

Social ministry refers to helping persons with spiritual, physical, emotional, mental, and relational problems in the name of Christ. Anne Davis, former dean of the Carver School of Church Social Work at The Southern Baptist Theological Seminary, defines social ministry as "the activities carried out by redeemed individuals, called by God to proclaim the good news, to minister to the needy, and to seek justice for all."[1]

Her definition has some attractive characteristics. First, it emphasizes the fact that social ministry is a process carried out by redeemed individuals. Others may provide social services and show compassion for persons in need, but social ministry is uniquely the function of persons who are born again according to God's redemptive grace. Second, it emphasizes that those who perform social ministry functions do so as a result of God's specific calling. When humanistic motivation has run its course, the Christian who, in grateful obedience to God's redeeming grace, responds to God's call will have access to a source of strength and compassion not available to the unredeemed.

For the purposes of this book, *social ministry* is "an organized process used by redeemed individuals who are called by God to proclaim the good news, demonstrating Christ's concern for the spiritual, physical, emotional, mental, and relational well-being of persons, families, groups, and communities both inside and outside the community of faith." The process is organized because effective helping is rational and orderly. It is process rather than product oriented; the most important part of ministry is found in the relationship between the helper and the one needing help.[2] The methods used by the helper will be determined by an interface among the minister, agency resources, and the needs of persons being helped.

Social ministry emphasizes the demonstration of Christlike concern because Jesus is our model for helping persons in need. He not only taught us that we should be concerned; He demonstrated the type of concern we are to have. He did more than inspire this type of concern; He commanded it. This concern always expresses itself in concrete action. The goal of social ministry has to do with helping persons in the Spirit of Christ.

Focus and Targets

The focus of social ministry is the spiritual, physical, emotional, mental, and relational needs of human beings. These are the very needs we are commanded to meet when we love God and our

---

[1]C. Anne Davis, "The Practice of Urban Ministry: Christian Social Ministries," *Review and Expositor*, 80, (1983): 523-536.

[2]Alan Keith-Lucas, *Giving and Taking Help* (Chapel Hill: University of North Carolina Press, 1972), 3-19.

neighbor as ourselves. We are told that by these criteria the nations will be judged. "Inasmuch as ye have done it unto one of the least of these my brethren, ye have done it unto me" (Matt. 25:40, KJV). In addition, this kind of helping is even to include our enemies.

The targets of this active concern are individuals, families, groups, and communities. Individuals become the focus of all ministry because, in the final analysis, any effective ministry must ultimately come down to one human being helping another. In that sense it is personal, just as our relationship with the Lord is personal. Ministry is with families because the basic unit of human society is the family. The well-being of families is essential to the well-being of individuals and the well-being of the church. Ministry is with groups and communities because the Christian is a part of humanity and is involved in groups in society. This is especially true of the community in which the person lives, works, plays, and worships. This ministry is to persons both inside and outside the community of faith. In Galatians 6:10 we are told to "do good unto all [persons], especially unto them who are of the household of faith" (KJV). The New Testament teaches us to be responsible for our fellow believers and to love our enemies in the same way (Rom. 12:14-21). Jesus is our primary model for this type of ministry. The early church spread the gospel throughout the world by following His example.

When persons are experiencing stress, problems, crisis, or disability, God's people have traditionally gathered around them to help. These needs have generally originated with some dysfunction in one or more of the domains of life: spiritual, mental, emotional, physical, economic, or relational. The spiritual domain has to do with the ability of the person to celebrate wholeness or completeness in the presence and work of God in his or her life which results in a growing and satisfying relationship with God and God's church, people, Word, and creation. The mental and emotional domains of life refer to education, reasoning, problem solving, and emotional stability. The physical domain includes health or the absence or control of diseases affecting the body. Income, savings, and employment are factors in the economic domain. The relational domain includes family, friends, and community.

Christian Social Ministry as Social Work

Social ministry uses most of the knowledge and skills used in professional social work. However, social work is by definition a secular profession. Many Christian professional social workers are employed by churches, judicatories or associations, and denominationally related agencies in the delivery of social services. When these social workers are thus employed, they become social ministers. Other persons who have training and experience in the field of social service delivery may also be employed as social ministers.

Social ministry shares many values with professional social work. However, social ministry is older than professional social work. The social work profession had its beginnings in the social ministries of churches and religiously oriented charities of Europe and America. Most social workers agree that the values of the social work profession are derived from the "Judeo-Christian ethic." This phrase refers to the concepts of righteousness, justice, and grace as they are revealed in the Old and New Testaments. God's righteousness demands that we practice justice in our relationships. Justice is conceived of as the practice of caring for the hungry, the thirsty, the stranger, the sick, and the oppressed or imprisoned. When used as a verb, grace is the delivery of unconditional services to any person who is in need. Another word for the practice of justice and grace is *help*.

Jewish and Christian ethics are not the only approaches people have taken to helping. Some of the earliest organized helping was practiced by the ancient Egyptians. In Egyptian society concern for persons had to do with their physical condition. Thus, for Egyptians, the supplying of material things, including equipping the dead with items to aid them in their continuing existence, was an act of worship of one or more gods. Ancient Greek and Roman societies also had distinct approaches to helping. However, Jewish and Christian teachings have made the greatest contributions to contemporary humanitarian approaches to helping.

Christian Social Ministry as Ministry

Growing out of a biblical and theological foundation, the philosophy of social ministry marks out the path for an effective, Christlike process of helping. Social ministry is a calling, based upon Christlike compassion. As such, it is ingrained in the four basic functions of the church: worship, evangelism, education, and ministry.

Some have referred to social ministry as "demonstration evangelism." Through one's reaching out to those who are disenfranchised, sick, hungry, and otherwise indigent, the gospel of

grace is most clearly demonstrated. A gospel that does not demonstrate God's grace is empty and ineffective. In the same manner, a
social service that does not help persons deal with their need for a
saving relationship with Jesus Christ is not a ministry. It is only a
service.

The reason a person engages in the process of helping others
is very important. For Christians, the love of humanity is not
enough. Our individual capacity to love is limited and is no more
effective than secular humanism if it is our primary resource.
Grateful obedience to the will of God is our primary motive for
engaging in social ministry. We are to be instruments of God's love.
Therefore, we depend upon God's capacity to help us help others.

The life-style of the social minister is crucial to his or her
effectiveness as a helper. Sensitivity to racial and ethnic differences
can aid or hinder a minister. Gender relationships are also very
important. Our attitude to personal morality is very valuable. It is
important that the social minister respect and honor persons who
are different, but not let those differences adversely affect the helping process. When working with persons who are engaged in sinful
activities, the minister must be capable of separating the sin from
the sinner.

Using the theoretical framework of contemporary social
work practice, social ministry develops skills and methods that
effectively help persons who are experiencing some forms of dysfunction in their lives. The basis for accepting or rejecting theoretical frameworks is predicated on their compatibility with biblical
principles. The essential skills of information gathering, assessment, planning, implementation, evaluation, termination, and
aftercare are discussed. These skills are generic to all forms of helping.

Programs of Christian Social Ministry

Social ministers are called upon to work with various levels
of systems. Methods of direct intervention with individuals, families, and groups are basic: these are called *microsystem interventions*.
Methods of ministry that call for working with neighborhoods,
communities, agencies, and organizations are referred to as *macrosystem interventions*.

Social ministers are called upon to perform many roles in
helping. At times they act as case managers, brokers, or counselors.
At other times they will serve as educators, advocates, social plan-

ners, consultants, or evangelists. For the most part, social ministers function as generalists.

Social ministry program development can be divided into three categories. *Enrichment* includes programs and services enabling persons who are already in a state of well-being to grow and improve the qualities of their lives. *Prevention* includes programs and services that anticipate the deterioration of such persons who are at a risk of moving into a dysfunctional state of being. *Treatment* provides personal services to dysfunctional persons, families, groups, organizations, and communities, offering services which will move them toward a status of well-being.

Each chapter of this book will begin with a delineation of the chapter's goals and objectives. It will end with activities that will help the reader to measure the degree to which the objectives have been achieved. As each chapter's learning activities are completed, the reader is encouraged to move to the next. Chapter 1 will establish a historical foundation upon which contemporary social ministry programs may be built. Chapter 2 will address contemporary denominational and religious organizational approaches to social ministry. Chapter 3 will develop an Old and New Testament basis for social ministry. Chapter 4 will elucidate a systematic theological foundation for social ministry. Chapter 5 will provide a philosophy of social ministry for contemporary practice. Chapter 6 will outline the methods and skills that are essential for effective social ministry. Chapter 7 will provide information on the various roles performed by social ministers. Chapter 8 will elaborate on the scope of social ministry programming for the local church, judicatory, or church-related agency.

Chapter One

Historical Foundations for Christian Social Ministry

Goals: A study of this chapter should enable the social minister to understand . . .

1. how major civilizations have approached helping persons in need.
2. the contribution of church leaders to social ministry throughout history.
3. how churches throughout history have approached ministry to persons in need.
4. the breadth or scope of social ministry models practiced by churches and other organizations in ancient and recent history.

Objectives: The minister . . .

1. identifies differences among ancient Egyptian, Greek, Roman, Jewish, and Christian approaches to helping.
2. chronicles the contributions of church leaders throughout history to the development of contemporary social ministry.
3. identifies the changes in the church's approach to social ministry that took place during the Protestant Reformation.
4. describes the models of social ministry that were developed by the church in ancient and recent history.

In order for us to put social ministry into perspective as a function of the church, we should lay a historical cornerstone. It is important to understand that social ministry is not simply a creation of contemporary social activists, but the work of God. This has been evident since the creation of human beings. Social ministry has always been a practice of God's people throughout history. It will be helpful for us to see how social ministry was viewed and implemented in both the Jewish and the early Christian heritage.

Ancient Models of Helping

Social ministry as a major function of the people of God has ancient historical roots. The formation of societies, both ancient and modern, testify to the fact that humans have always been at least as interested in helping each other as they have been in destroying one another. The principle of mutual assistance and the responsibility of the strong to protect and provide for the weak—especially within the limited, intimate groups such as the family and tribe—has been established in almost all societies from ancient times.[1]

Although hostility and oppression have been found in most primitive and ancient tribes, there seems to have always been a plan for helping those in need. The method of selecting the recipients of this help is not always clear, and when it is, it is not always altruistic. In some societies the weak, infirm, crippled, and aged are cast out, killed, or neglected. This is especially true if they are not members of the "right group." It is said that some Eskimo tribes have traditionally encouraged their elderly and infirm, who can no longer contribute to the survival of the group, to voluntarily isolate themselves on an ice floe. They are carried out to sea or become victims of an attack by animals seeking food. In this way they make a final contribution to the survival of their families and friends. Other primitive peoples share similar experiences in their cultural histories.

Different contemporary societies have developed various philosophies of helping. Some of these are basically altruistic, and some are very conditional. For most societies, the reasons for helping have religious significance. This significance has generally led to formalizing the process of helping. In the ancient primitive tribes, the *shaman* (medicine man) became the specialist in helping. In the Jewish experience, the priests and rabbis became the special-

---

[1]Haskel Miller, *Compassion and Community* (New York: Association Press, 1961), 22.

ists. In the Christian church, priests, pastors, and other ministers have traditionally been viewed as the specialists in helping.

The Ancient Egyptian System

Ancient writings indicate that Egyptians felt strongly that the gods must be respected and honored. The gods were seen as the source of all life. Demonstration of this respect involved the managing of physical and material things. Thus, the primary concern for helping had to do with the person's physical and material needs.

Vonhoff identified seven acts of mercy carried out by the Egyptian people. They are very similar to those listed in both the Old and New Testaments. These acts of mercy are not contained in any one document, but gleaned from the writings of the priests of several gods. However, they appear to be consistently honored even by contemporary Egyptians.[2]

The first act of mercy had to do with the *relief of the hungry*. References are made in the Egyptian priests' writings to building granaries and dispensing grain to the needy during periods of great famine. Persons are admonished to feed the hungry. The Egyptian might kill an enemy with a gun or knife, but he would not allow him to starve to death.

The second work of mercy had to do with *relief of the thirsty*. In Egypt, as in the whole geographical region, water has always been considered an important commodity. It was a moral crime to allow a person to go thirsty. This merciful act was also extended to one's enemies.

Relief of the naked was the third act of mercy. A prominent inscription on the walls of some tombs in Egypt describes the entombed person's honorable act of "clothing the naked" or "giving shelter to the naked."

Help for the stranger was the fourth act of mercy ascribed to the ancient Egyptian system. Even one's enemies were to be fed and protected while in the home of an Egyptian. A traveler in need would be given any possible aid. The homeless were not left to fend for themselves.

The fifth act of mercy was the *relief of prisoners*. Prisoners were to be visited, prayed for, and treated kindly. Although Egyptians have always had prisons for the lawless, they did not like to imprison persons. One of the inscriptions about a great Pharaoh says that he performed the honorable act of emptying the prisons.

---

[2]Heinz Vonhoff, *People Who Care* (Philadelphia: Fortress Press, 1960), 1-6.

Care of the sick was the sixth act of mercy. All possible assistance was to be given to the sick, the crippled, and the mentally ill. This practice led to some of the greatest advancements in ancient medicine by Egyptian physicians.

The last and seventh act of mercy was the *care of the dead*. The departed person was rendered every possible service. He was to be provided with every earthly need and kept in his present state as long as possible. This practice led to the development of the process of embalming.

The Ancient Greek System

For the ancient Greek, helping others furthered the development of his own soul. Although helping was altruistic to some extent, essentially it was self-serving. Helping was readily extended to one's equals, but those of lower estate were ignored for the most part.[3]

Meeting the needs of those who were in crisis or dysfunctional also had theological implications. For the ancient Greek, a god was an example or an ideal. Gods were beyond the reach of humans and unmoved by humanity's fortunes or misfortunes. The nearer the Greek came to being like a god, the more acts of mercy were considered to be a weakness and unworthy of the person. If the gods decided to create hardships and sufferings, mortals were to bear them philosophically and with dignity.

The attitude of the ancient Greek included a judgment of the worthiness of the one being helped and how this would affect the helper. One could be considerate and helpful to another of equal or higher estate. However, to give aid to one of lower estate would be an unworthy act. Also, it was unacceptable to help a person of equal estate if that person had gotten into trouble by behaving in an unworthy manner.

For example, it is reported that Aristotle was observed giving alms to such a person one day. He was promptly confronted by another philosopher who stated that the man was not worthy. For the Greek, giving help to the unworthy was not considered a good deed. Aristotle's answer was, "I had mercy on the man, not on his bad morals. To give to one's fellowman is indeed good: it is an act worthy of an excellent and honorable man." Although there is a

---

[3]Alan Keith-Lucas, *Giving and Taking Help* (Chapel Hill: University of North Carolina Press, 1972), 183-199.

certain amount of nobility in this attitude, the motive remains primarily selfish.[4]

The Ancient Roman System

It appears that the ancient Romans took care of their own—that is, their dependents—and particularly those who gave them service in return. They defined those who were worthy of help as anyone who lived beneath their roof or within their district and were politically relevant to their aspirations. This help was to be rational and selective.[5] Vonhoff recounted Seneca's contention that pity is only for "old wives." He would help those who weep, but he saw no need to weep with them. He helped because it was rational to do so and because good deeds make for a good conscience.[6]

The Jewish System

Probably the oldest formalized program of justice, kindness, and mercy is the Jewish system. Numerous passages in the Old Testament give both commandment and example to the Jewish people regarding justice, kindness, and mercy. The orphan, widow, stranger, slave, divorcee, aged, sick, and hungry were provided for (Ex. 22:25-27; Lev. 14:21-32; Deut. 15:1-11; 24:1-4; Isa. 1:1-31; Amos 2:6; 5:11-12; 8:4-6).

God's primary concern was for mercy, justice, and love, as opposed to religious ritual and ceremony (Jer. 5:25-29; Ezek. 18; Hosea 6:6; Amos 5:21-24; Mic. 6:6-8).[7] At the heart of Jewish theology, God is seen as an absolutely ethical being. Because of this the Hebrews developed an acute awareness of their own responsibility in their relationships with one another.[8]

Throughout the Old Testament, kindness, mercy, and giving to the poor are associated with the just disposition of disputes and man's general relationship with those less fortunate. Justice is mentioned twice as often as kindness or mercy; even in Micah's summation of God's requirements, justice is mentioned first (Mic. 6:8).[9] An examination of Old Testament passages reveals that there are 105 references to justice, 32 to compassion, and 21 to kindness; and

---

[4]Vonhoff, *People Who Care*, 6-8.

[5]Keith-Lucas, *Giving and Taking Help*, 185-199.

[6]Vonhoff, *People Who Care*, 1-10.

[7]William Pinson, *Applying the Gospel: Suggestions for Christian Social Action in a Local Church* (Nashville: Broadman Press, 1975), 1-16.

[8]Miller, *Compassion and Community*, 24.

[9]Keith-Lucas, *Giving and Taking Help*, 185-199.

many of these specifically refer to actions toward those less fortunate.[10]

The Unique Christian Contribution

Christians share the ethical traditions of the Jews. The Jewish Bible is contained in the Christian Bible as the Old Testament. For the Christian, the ethical directives of the Old Testament are just as binding as any portion of the New Testament. These directives are not in competition, but they are complementary with New Testament ethical teachings. Rising out of these traditions is the additional quality of *agape* love. This type of love is not a romantic attachment, but a valuing, thinking-well-of, commitment to the well-being of the other person.[11]

Perhaps the most unique contribution of Christianity to the concept of social ministry is its emphasis upon a God-inspired and God-empowered concern for every person. (This concept will be discussed in more detail in chapter 3.) The Christian perceives social ministry as an expression of God's concern for any person who is in need. The question "Who is worthy of help?" is answered by the Christian's recognition of the worth and uniqueness of every human being because each is important to God.

Most Christians know that they cannot love everybody. However, they feel responsible for doing what they can to help persons in need. They serve these persons out of grateful obedience to God's will. Feeling that every Christian is a recipient of God's grace, therefore indebted to Him, they are constrained to do what God wants, regardless of their personal feelings toward specific person(s) in need. As with the Egyptians, this even includes their enemies.

The Ancient and Medieval Church

Members of the early Christian church took Jesus seriously in trying to express love in a manner consistent with His example and teachings. No other group has contributed so much to the concept of helping. The actions and teachings of the early Christian churches are evidences of this fact. They sold their property and gave to each other as the need arose (Acts 2:44-45); therefore, because of this there were no destitute persons among them (Acts

---

[10]Alan Keith-Lucas, *The Poor You Have With You Always* (St. Davids, Penn.: North American Association of Christians in Social Work, 1989), 6.
[11]Ibid.

4:34). The strong were taught to help the weak without being judgmental (Rom. 15:1-2; Gal. 6:1). By doing so they would be fulfilling the "law of Christ" (Gal. 6:2).

The Passive Change Agent Ministry Model

Although Christians are taught to be especially sensitive to the plight of fellow Christians, they are admonished to be concerned with all persons (Gal. 6:9-10; 1 Thess. 3:12; 5:15). There was always an emphasis on evangelism. This kept the door to the bosom of the fellowship open to "whosoever will."[12] Even during the periods of great persecution when they were considered a scourge upon the earth by Jews and Gentiles alike, Christians distinguished themselves by putting this concern into action and thus gaining great sympathy, acclaim, and strength for their cause.[13]

Following the example of Jesus, the early church responded to whatever human needs they could meet in whatever way they could meet them. They engaged in at least ten areas of social ministry: care of widows and orphans; care of the sick, poor, and disabled; care of prisoners and captives; burial of the poor and other dead; care of slaves; care of victims of calamity; employment services; hospitality and agape meals.[14]

Bakke discussed "cemetery and trash heap evangelism," describing how Christians, during the first three centuries, would give proper burial to bodies left on city trash heaps and rescue children whom pagans threw on the trash heaps, taking them into their homes and raising them as their own.[15] This practice could have been the earliest form of Christian foster care. They became known for their courageous and sacrificial relief work. Observers were amazed at how Christians ministered to everyone without favor, in times of plague or public calamity. In Carthage during a series of epidemics, Christians stayed and ministered to the sick and dying even when pagan families had fled in panic. In Alexandria women rounded up destitute babies and orphans and cared for them. Christians in Egyptian cities would hear of a sick family and offer to move in to nurse them, deliberately exposing themselves to illness.[16]

---

[12]Miller, *Compassion and Community*, 30.

[13]Thomas B. Maston, "Baptists, Social Christianity, and American Culture," *Review and Expositor* (1964).

[14]E. Glenn Hinson, "The Historical Involvement of the Church in Social Ministries and Social Action," *Review and Expositor*, 85, no. 2 (Spring 1978): 233-236.

[15]Ray Bakke, *Urban Christian* (Downers Grove, Ill.: InterVarsity Press, 1987), 83-85.

[16]Ibid., 83.

Latourette stated that the Christian concept of sharing and concern differed from the charity tradition of the Greco-Roman world in three significant ways: (1) it increased the number of givers, (2) it modified the motive, and (3) it altered the form of the help.[17] The number of givers was increased because in the Greco-Roman cultures, only the few who were wealthy or endowed with status were expected to contribute, while in the Christian faith, everyone was allowed to participate in helping those who were less fortunate. Selfish motives were put aside for the exercise of *agape* in grateful obedience to God and in response to His love. The form of help became personal and unselfish, based on the need of the person rather than on any benefit it might accrue for the helper.

This became the characteristic behavior of almost all Christian missionaries. They not only went all over the known world proclaiming the message of Christ as the forgiver of sins and the Savior of humanity, but they also demonstrated Christ's love by their concern for every person's need as they encountered him or her. This compassion for suffering humanity was probably the most significant action of early Christians. It led to the rapid spread of the gospel throughout all of the known world during the first three centuries.[18]

Tertullian wrote in his *Anthology* in A.D. 200: "To no less a post than this has God called them, and they dare not try to evade it. We have filled up every place belonging to you—islands, castles, caves, prisons, palace, city forum. We leave you with your temples only." The early church reached out to other cultures, surrounding them at many different levels. Bakke observed that we do not need new technologies to reach the city for Christ; we only need to rediscover this vision, energy, and compassion.[19]

Constantine's conversion to Christianity proved to be a great boost to the social ministry of the early churches. The emperor supplied funding to a wide range of social projects and supported legislation that reflected Christian social views. Wealthy persons were encouraged to follow his example. Early Christians did not embark on a campaign against slavery, but slaves were accepted by the church. Some slaves were included with the martyrs, and some became ordained ministers. By Constantine's time the imperial code regarding slavery had already begun to reflect some Christian influence. In fact, Constantine and subsequent leaders of Rome

---

[17]Kenneth S. Latourette, "The First Five Centuries," *A History of the Expansion of Christianity*, vol. 6 (New York: Harper and Brothers, 1937), 265-268.
[18]Ibid.
[19]Bakke, *Urban Christian*, 83.

began to shift matters of social significance toward the church leaders, even entrusting the bishops with judicial powers.

Emperor Julian attempted to revive paganism, using the Christian model of social ministry. He thought that everyone was turning to Christianity because "where Jews took care of their own and pagans took care of nobody, Christians took care of everybody, not only their own but the pagan needy as well."[20]

Thomas Aquinas, while placing an emphasis upon justice, recognized a moral debt to the poor and unfortunate. His main contribution to the process of social ministry was his emphasis on prudence or rational action, involving a relationship of the strong with the weak. He is quoted as saying, "It is only insofar as we are superior to others that we can be of help to them, supplying their needs." His insistence on the uniqueness of each individual and the necessity for man to try to understand himself has been one of the basic cornerstones of modern social ministry.[21]

One of the major social ministry programs of the early church was help for the unemployed. This was very rational as well as practical. For many, becoming a Christian meant that one could no longer work in his or her vocation. Gladiators, prostitutes, actors, and others were being converted and the early church required that they no longer practice these trades. In order to care for them and others who lost their jobs as a result of becoming Christian or of economic decline, Christians attempted to create employment opportunities in a more acceptable vocation. Hinson stated that when the Empire became Christian, the churches were in a stronger position to provide for the unemployed. The monasteries provided employment for many. They coupled work with prayer, and these were seen as the twin pillars upon which communal monasticism rested. Not all of the persons in the monasteries were ordained clergy. There was a group called the lower clergy. Although they were technically recognized as ministers, they were unordained. Most of these were enrolled by the churches, more for the purpose of giving aid than for the work they might do.[22] Before Constantine's conversion this activity was considered illegal, but afterward it was not only legal but encouraged.

Under Christian influence the state took a more active interest in organizing charity programs. Social policy was also influenced to the extent that laws were passed to abolish crucifixion,

---

[20]Hinson, "The Historical Involvement of the Church," 236-238.
[21]Keith-Lucas, *Giving and Taking Help*, 185-199.
[22]Ibid.

encourage the liberation of slaves, discourage infanticide and divorce, and prohibit gladiatorial shows and games. Other policies showing increasing sympathy for the weak and unfortunate were implemented as well.[23]

The Enculturated Ministry Model

Although everything seemed to be going well for Christianity, the early church was not without confusion about what it meant to fulfill the "law of Christ." Along with their acceptance by the Roman Empire under Constantine came a form of success and influence that entrapped many. Instead of continuing as "change agents," a description that characterized their earlier efforts, they became subtly influenced by the Greco-Roman culture. As the church grew and became changed by the dominant culture, it began to differentiate between the sacred and the secular. Conflicting motives for charity clouded their witness and direct personal charity gave way to formal programs of assistance administered by bishops and other officials, many of whom advocated a judgment of the "worthy" poor and the "unworthy" poor heretofore unknown in the church.[24]

Three heresies arose which continue to persist even today. One of them was that to help those in need was a way to earn salvation. Cyprian taught that charity is "needful for the weak"—for which he might be commended—but also "glorious for the strong, assisted by which the Christian accomplishes spiritual grace, deserves well of Christ the judge, accounts God his debtor." The second heresy arose over establishing criteria for determining who was worthy of charity. Apparently the cities were full of persons who made begging an art. Basil indicated that it took great experience to distinguish between those who were really poor and those who begged only in order to collect money. The third heresy was to reduce the poor to an inferior class both socially and morally. They were considered socially inept and were not included in the larger society simply because they were poor. Their poverty was considered to be the result of some sin; therefore, they were assumed to be immoral.

This became the basis of social welfare policies. It remains the basis of contemporary social assistance policies in western societies. This is not only true of governmental programs of relief, but of church practices as well.[25]

---

[23]Miller, *Compassion and Community*, 31.
[24]Alan Keith-Lucas, *The Church and Social Welfare* (Philadelphia: Westminster Press, 1962), 19.
[25]Ibid., 18-32.

One strong leader who attempted to reflect the original spirit of Christian helping was Chrysostom. Toward the end of the fourth century he wrote, "Be we as large-hearted as we may, we shall never be able to contribute such love towards man as we stand in need of at the hand of God that loveth man." Keith-Lucas noted that Chrysostom was able to see what few can see even today: when a person asks for something he doesn't need, it may be an indication that he is actually in need in other ways. Chrysostom was unwilling to restrict aid to special groups. He would give to anyone in need, irrespective of their residence or their acceptability to the local church.[26] Chrysostom is quoted as saying, "The poor have only one recommendation: their need. If he be the most perverse of all men, should he lack necessary food we ought to appease his hunger."[27]

From its inception Christian social ministry represented no broad revolutionary program for social reform. No great effort was made to radically change the structure of society. Rather, Christians sought to show love and arouse a love response from those who were helped. Social ministry existed for this purpose rather than for correcting social wrongs. Early Christians believed that love, operating through persons in their relationship with one another, would effect all necessary changes.

Selfless devotion to helping the prisoners, the poor, the sick, and other unfortunate persons continued throughout the Middle Ages. This continued to be the mark of the ideal Christian. However, the organized church of the Middle Ages sought to become a comprehensive, unifying whole, embracing political and social institutions along with religion.[28] In so doing, it became identified with the oppressive actions of government and often played the role of the oppressor.

Hinson observed that inevitably a church so entangled in the fabric of society tends to lose contact with the needs of the people and thus alienate even its own. A number of social movements arose in protest to the apostasy of the organized church leadership. A significant number of these represented peasants and unskilled workers in the newly developing towns that began dotting the European landscape around A.D. 1100-1200. From time to time, significant voices were raised in objection and attempted to call the church back to its basic doctrines. One such person was Arnold of

---

[26]Keith-Lucas, *Giving and Taking Help*, 185-199.
[27]Keith-Lucas, *The Church and Social Welfare*, 21.
[28]Miller, *Compassion and Community*, 32-38.

Brescia (1155). He insisted that the church surrender its worldly power and possessions, becoming the church of the poor, and that the clergy subsist on tithes and voluntary offerings.[29]

Another significant voice was that of Peter Waldo. A friend had died suddenly in Lyons in 1176. Waldo sought the advice of a priest, who advised him to follow Christ's injunction to the rich young ruler. He immediately hired two priests to translate the Gospels into the vernacular and began to gather followers who would go out in pairs to preach. The followers became known as the "Waldenses" and were dubbed the "Poor Men of Lyons" at the Synod of Verona in 1184.

The Beguines, an association of devout women, originated around 1177. They lived semimonastic lives in houses which members supported by spinning, weaving, caring for the sick, and performing other social services.

These movements were comparable to the "liberation" movement in Latin America. The church in Latin America was less a target of protest because it had much less power and influence than the European church of the Middle Ages.[30]

The Institutional Model

Early in the Christian church's existence, concern for the sick, the uneducated, and the disenfranchised was acute. Schools were started, hospitals were built and staffed, and a number of monasteries served as places of refuge and work and provided various types of assistance for persons in need. Initially, these services were designed for members of the church. However needy pagans were not turned away.

One of the best-known institutions of mercy of the early-church period was the Xenodochium—a hospital and hospice—built during the fourth century by Basil, Bishop of Caesarea. Around the main building was a colony of separate units for strangers, the sick, and the poor. Even lepers had a house of their own there. A whole city of mercy came into being later known as the *Basileiad*, after its founder. Basil was able to raise a significant amount of money in support of his institution. The emperor Valens, who didn't like the bishop anyway, threatened to strip Basil of his fortune. Basil answered, "My fortune? Take this worn-out robe and

---

[29]Hinson, "The Historical Involvement of the Church," 239.
[30]Ibid.

my books. More I do not own!" He had never used any of the money that he had raised for anything but the hospital.[31]

When Basil died on January 1, 379, Gregory Nazianzen stated in his eulogy, "Go to the gates of the city and see the city of mercy, the storerooms of godliness, the treasure house of love, where the abundance of the rich and the pennies of the poor are gathered, where love is practiced, compassion demonstrated, and suffering exalted. Basil taught us to lend our mercy to God, just as we ourselves are in need of God's mercy."[32]

During the last half of the fourth century and the early part of the fifth century, many Christians began to retreat from the cities and form what were called "islands of mercy." They became monks in sequestered monasteries; they withdrew to hermitages, where they hoped to live in righteousness before their Lord. However, they did not perceive their withdrawal from the temptations of the cities as a withdrawal from their neighbors. Most of these monasteries maintained a hostel or hospital; in the lands of the Euphrates, Thalassius and his monks gathered and sheltered the blind beggars; in the desert of Scete, houses were built and work was provided for strangers.[33]

While there is some evidence that hospitals were first organized under Julian the Apostate rather than under Christian auspices, it was nevertheless true that the most significant development of the hospital movement occurred in the sixth century under Christian auspices. At times the inspiration for the movement came from the church's hierarchy and at other times from the monasteries.

In addition, the development of institutional charity moved consistently through the Middle Ages. This was true even at a time when the church bordered on, if not attained, complete corruption.

Although the monastic movement was essentially individualistic and indifferent to social problems at the societal level, it nevertheless represented a tremendous social and philanthropic activity. The poor were fed, the peasant was instructed in agriculture, the arts were kept alive, and education was developed within monastic walls.[34]

---

[31]Vonhoff, *People Who Care*, 24-25.
[32]Ibid., 25-26.
[33]Ibid., 30.
[34]Reinhold Niebuhr, *The Contribution of Religion to Social Work* (New York: Columbia University Press, 1932), 6.

The Reformation

As a reaction to the reluctance of the church to champion the cause of the poor, the powerless, and the destitute, and because the church was also perceived as corrupt and oppressive, the Reformation was born. The emphasis upon the worth of the individual and upon personal responsibility should have liberated persons' impulses to help others. Instead, they began to identify God's grace with worldly success and created a separate class of the poor. Although mention was often made of the "deserving poor" as opposed to the "undeserving poor," most poor persons were generally classified as undeserving.[35]

The Church-State Cooperation Model

Martin Luther, recognizing that the scattered and irregular efforts of local groups were inadequate, appealed to German governmental leaders in 1520 to take responsibility for the poor and to establish a "common chest" for receiving regular contributions for the relief of the needy. Luther realized that many were not being helped by the monastic system. He came to believe that the churches could not deal with such a massive problem and that the state had a responsibility for all its citizens. Church and state working together, he felt, could assist all of those who truly needed help. This combination would also address some of the issues of corruption that were rampant in the existing system. The plan was implemented, marking the beginning of the church's practice of shifting a significant portion of the care of the needy to the state, in 1525. Ulrich Zwingli carried out a similar plan in Zurich.[36]

The Social Action Model

The Reformation did revive interest in individual responsibility and adherence to the Word of God. The framework was there for a truly biblical approach to ministry, and in some instances it actually did pick up the original form. Protestantism's impulse "to recapture the spirit of the religion of Jesus" was not expressed, however, in the pattern of the monastics. Monastics tended toward withdrawal from society and ministry to the many who were victims of social ills. Protestants, on the other hand, while not refraining from some forms of direct social ministry, exerted an influence

---

[35]Keith-Lucas, *Giving and Taking Help*, 185-199.
[36]Walter A. Friedlander, *Introduction to Social Welfare* (Englewood Cliffs: Prentice-Hall, 1968), 10.

more in the direction of attacking social ills through reform movements. They sought to alter the social institutions and social patterns causing the hurt. In this manner they would relieve distress for the many rather than the few; they would attempt to break the recurring patterns of social ills that shaped the policies of church and state alike.[37]

The Church Parsonage Model

While Luther, Calvin, and Zwingli struggled to establish purity in doctrine and moral behavior, their plans for a systematic program for caring for the needy were not being implemented in an effective manner. However, many programs of mercy were being developed by individual Protestant pastors and churches.

Matthaus and Katharina Zell were prime examples. In 1522 they were married and established the first official Protestant church parsonage in Strasbourg. It immediately became a haven for needy and persecuted people although this was not its stated purpose. At this time many people were being denied access to their own homes for religious and other political reasons. Hundreds of them came to Strasbourg. Katharina took care of fifty to sixty refugees per day in her home. She helped others find food and shelter and wrote letters to their families. Matthaus and Katharina made appeals for aid, collected provisions, and saw to the distribution to the needy. Shortly before her own death, she performed funerals for persons who were not of the faith of any of the churches in the city. Matthaus was out of town, and she could not find a pastor who would perform the ceremony. The Strasbourg parsonage was the prototype and became the model of Protestant parsonages for generations to come.[38]

The Diaconate Model

In the wake of the persecutions during the Reformation, some congregational reforms took place which reached back to the formation of deacons and deaconesses in the New Testament. Jan Laski, a Polish nobleman and minister, was driven out of his homeland. He was given asylum in England by Edward VI. Dutch refugees formed a church and Laski became their pastor. He gave them a set of bylaws, which included the naming of deacons and deaconesses who dedicated themselves totally to serving the needy. The

---

[37]Miller, *Compassion and Community*, 41-42.
[38]Vonhoff, *People Who Care*, 86-94.

basis for their work was stated in a report dated 1594: "Since God has made man body and soul, he has also, in his divine wisdom and grace, provided and prescribed the framework and the needs of each part. Hence, there is ordained and commanded in the Old and New Testament, besides the preaching office, the *diaconiae pauperum* or ministries to the poor."

The deacons instituted a house-to-house mission to the poor. Thirty-two deacons would visit needy people in their homes. The city was divided into six districts, and every Saturday afternoon the deacons met, parceled out assignments, exchanged experiences, and dealt with complaints. All income and expenses were recorded. Any beggar who knocked on the door was referred to the appropriate deacon. A foster-care program was instituted whereby townspeople would take young boys into their homes in order to give them an education in school or to apprentice them in a trade. They also hired a barber/surgeon to doctor the sick. In addition they set up a ministry to seamen, not only to needy sailors but also for all shipwrecked sailors.[39]

Another, perhaps even more prominent, deaconess program was begun under the leadership of Theodore Fliedner, a Lutheran pastor in Kaiserswerth, Germany. He began a refuge for discharged women convicts and expanded it into a hospital to care for the sick. He is credited with being the first in the Protestant tradition to bring together and train church women as deaconesses who had pledged to give their lives to nursing and social work. It was this program that inspired Florence Nightingale. In this way he influenced the beginnings of modern nursing. Many congregations of various church traditions in both Europe and America continue to employ the deaconess/church social worker to this day.[40]

On the whole, the Protestant Reformation contributed four significant emphases that continue to influence the practice of social ministry by Christian churches today: (1) encouraging the general public, both governmental and private, to assume responsibility for persons in need; (2) encouraging private volunteerism and church benevolence based on a sincere response to the love of God; (3) encouraging persons to practice thrift and industry as a means of pleasing God and thus providing for oneself; and (4) engaging in social reform, in a limited way, as a means of correcting some of the more glaring social evils.[41]

---

[39]Ibid.
[40]Miller, *Compassion and Community,* 45.
[41]Ibid.

The Daughters of Charity

Although not a part of the *Protestant* Reformation, a very significant development in the Catholic Church deserves mention here. It is referred to in the literature as "The Daughters of Charity," "The Daughters of Mercy," or the "Ladies of Charity." It was begun by one of the most important Catholic reformers during the period of the Counter-Reformation, Father Vincent de Paul, in France. He had been captured by Tunisian pirates and sold as a galley slave. Because of this experience, after he escaped he devoted his life to the improvement of the destitute, especially prisoners and their families, orphans, illegitimate children, and the sick and hungry.

He organized a lay order, the Ladies of Charity, who visited the poor in their homes and distributed food and clothing. In 1633 he founded the Daughters of Charity, composed of young women from poor families who were trained in nursing and serving the poor. They became the forerunners of modern Catholic social caseworkers. He had tried to organize a group of wealthy women earlier, but they were reluctant to visit in the homes and communities of the poor. Many of his other ideas caused important reforms to be made in the charity programs under Catholic auspices.[42]

The Modern Church

In the aftermath of the Industrial Revolution which had spurred such acts as the Statute of Laborers and later the Poor Law, a proliferation of charitable organizations attempted to provide assistance to the displaced farm laborers and others who began to swell the already overpopulated ghettoes in the industrial centers.

Many farms had been turned into pastureland, and machinery was doing the work of many men. Industry was looking for skilled workmen and machinists and these farmers could not qualify for the jobs that were available. Conditions were often unsafe, and many able-bodied men became injured and unable to work. Disease-infested ghettoes caused the death of many parents. This occurrence gave rise to large numbers of orphaned children who had no alternative but to beg and steal in order to survive.

While the Poor Law and its predecessors attempted to alleviate conditions, it was often administered in such a way as to cause more hurt than it alleviated. The programs carried out by the churches and other private organizations seemed to duplicate

---

[42]Vonhoff, *People Who Care*, 97-103.

17

many services and completely ignore others. Often services were too limited to be effective in areas where the needs were great.

The Charity Organization Society

In 1814 Thomas Chalmers, a Presbyterian minister, was called to be the minister of the parish of St. John's in Glasgow, Scotland. It was one of the poorest in the city. For years he had detested the Poor Law and its harsh administration, especially as he saw it in Glasgow. He organized his parish under the leadership of the deacons of his church. There were twenty-five units with one deacon in charge of each unit. Each unit consisted of fifty families. The deacon's job was to know each family and to investigate all requests for help coming from his unit. The first response the deacon would make was to encourage self-help, then help from the family, then from others, and ultimately from the well-to-do. A court of deacons served as a clearinghouse. They would review requests for help and make appropriate assignments. When problems were not resolved by the prescribed means, they would make suggestions to the appropriate deacon regarding the resolution of the case.[43]

Chalmers insisted that each deacon investigate with friendliness and provide personal service. This principle became the foundation upon which the Charity Organization Society of London was developed with its "Friendly Visitors." They were the forerunners of modern British social workers.[44] Many cities throughout the industrial world picked up on this idea, and other Charity Organization Societies soon began to appear.

Within four years after the founding of the London Charity Organization Society, America experienced a severe depression that added to the woes already present as a result of the Civil War. Various cities had adopted some of the ideas used in London, but there arose a need for a more concerted effort. Stephen Humphreys Gurteen, assistant rector of St. Paul's Church in Buffalo, New York, became the driving force and organizer of the first Charity Organization Society in America. He traveled to London and studied the system there. When he returned he called the first meeting in Buffalo in December 1877. Within six years the central principles of the charity organization movement had been adopted by twenty-five cities. The Friendly Visitors who worked for the various societies later became known as Social Caseworkers.

---

[43]Arthur Fink, Wilson Anderson, and Merrill Conover, *The Field of Social Work* (Dallas: Holt, Rinehart and Winston, 1968), 35-39.

[44]Keith-Lucas, *Giving and Taking Help*, 185-199.

The Settlement House Movement

Even when the Charity Organization Societies in London began providing better care for the individual, some local church leaders began to notice that certain pockets of poverty were not being affected. One of these leaders was Vicar (later Canon) Barnett who worked directly with the poor in London's notorious East End during the latter half of the nineteenth century. Another was a lecturer and tutor in theology at Oxford University, Arnold Toynbee (1852-1883). He lived in Whitechapel Parish with Barnett and his wife. They sought to improve the conditions of the poor and hopeless as well as to change the environment, which was working against them. Together they came up with the idea of purchasing a house in the midst of the settlement. It would become a residence for some educated (usually wealthy) persons, who could serve as examples, teachers, and providers of basic human services. They felt that this "settlement house" would be a useful instrument for dealing with the problems of poverty.[45]

Many young men, especially those preparing for the ministry, responded. In 1884, shortly after the death of Toynbee, the first settlement house was organized and became operational. It was named Toynbee Hall in honor of the young man who had given so much of his energy to assisting Barnett in the development of the concept.[46]

The social settlement idea spread throughout Great Britain. Along with Charles B. Stover, Stanton Coit founded the first settlement house in America in 1887. It was called the Neighborhood Guild of New York City. Taking a cue from Coit and Barnett, Jane Addams and Ellen Gates Starr founded Hull House in Chicago in 1889. Jane Addams' Hull House is probably the most well-known settlement house in American history, due to the tireless work of Addams. It is said that her office contained a slogan reading, "If not me, who? If not now, when?" She was actively involved in every facet of the community. Her work included working directly with individuals, families, and groups; using the settlement house to educate poor persons, both children and adults; and engaging in social action on behalf of the community. Although the settlement houses in Europe and America were the forerunners of modern secular group work, they had a strong Christian influence. Hull

---

[45]Lorene M. Pacey, ed., *Readings in the Development of Settlement Work* (New York: Association Press, 1950), 8-27.

[46]Fink, Anderson, and Conover, *The Field of Social Work*, 36-37.

House, for example, had Bible study groups as one of its primary educational activities.

Summary and Conclusions

This chapter has delineated some of the historical antecedents to contemporary social ministry. It has shown how persons in ancient times responded to the need of other human beings. It has demonstrated how the early church incorporated social ministry into everyday life as a part of its mission.

The early and medieval churches developed several models for social ministry such as the Enculturated Ministry Model and Institutional Model. The churches of the Reformation and post-Reformation Eras developed the Church-State Cooperation Model, the Social Action Model, the Church Parsonage Model, the Diaconate Model, and the Daughters of Charity model. Social service movements such as the Charity Organization Society and the Settlement House movement were discussed.

Heresies regarding worthy and unworthy persons in need were discussed. These heresies arose in the early church and continued to exist even after the Reformation. They came into being as a result of the churches' attempts to determine who should receive help and who should not.

The history of Christian social ministries is rich and varied. It is not separate from Christian history but is an integral part of it. From the beginning of creation, God's concern for humanity has been demonstrated in the Bible. His work with the men and women He has used to reveal Himself has always included concern for every person and every facet of humanity's existence. This is one of the chief foundation stones upon which programs of social ministry are built.

Exercises for Review and Examination

1. Compare and contrast the ancient Egyptian, Greek, and Roman approaches to helping with the Jewish and Christian approaches.

2. Write a two-page discussion of how the churches throughout history have treated the concept of the worth of all persons to receive help, regardless of how they came to be in need.

3. List and state one principle of ministry learned from each of the models of social ministry discussed in this chapter.

Chapter Two

Organizational Models for Christian Social Ministry

Goal: A study of this chapter should enable the social minister to understand the contributions made by various religious organizations and denominations to contemporary social ministry.

Objectives: The minister . . .

1. compares the approaches of Puritans and Quakers to social ministry.
2. describes two major themes that shaped American Evangelicals' approach to social ministry.
3. discusses how various American denominations integrate faith and social ministry.
4. identifies approaches to theological education for social ministry.

Growing out of a long history of practicing social ministries, churches, denominations, and other religious organizations have developed a wide array of ministry models. For some, the motivation for such services is purely humanitarian. Such ministries are developed because of concern for hurting humanity. Others, however, have ulterior motives for developing social ministry programs. For example, some social ministry programs are begun in order to evangelize a group of people as opposed to simply meeting their needs for food, clothing, or shelter. Still other programs are begun with both humanitarian and evangelistic motives.

The Puritans

When the term "Puritan" is used, many think only of rigid, self-righteous persons who were obsessed with sexual morality. However, the Puritans of the seventeenth century in both England and America were very concerned with social and economic justice. They did more than simply preach about the atrocities inflicted on poor and unsuspecting persons by the government and merchants of their day. The Puritans called upon "all good Christians" to stand up for those who had been deprived and abused by the social system. In America, one of their goals was to establish a colony based on "a legacy of social responsibility in the form of covenants." By this means citizens were sworn by an oath to care for one another.[1]

The Quakers

One of the major contributions to modern social ministry has been made by the Quakers. The Quaker doctrine of the "inner light" emphasizes the immense value of every individual. All persons are of value to God and should be treated as such. George Fox, the founder of the Society of Friends (Quakers), was an early proponent of prison reform. For him, every individual was a dwelling place of God, whether the person recognized it or not. Therefore, no one could be considered "lower class." For this reason the Quakers chose to use the informal "thee" instead of the formal "you"—not to sound like twelfth century England or the *King James Version* of the Bible, but to show their common concern for all persons. This attitude set the stage for the Quakers' ministries to the poor, prison reform, opposition to slavery, and pacifism.[2]

The Salvation Army

Growing out of the poverty and degradation left in the wake of the Industrial Revolution, various groups sprang up in Europe and America to deal with the massive problems. One such organization was the Salvation Army. The founders of the Army were William and Catherine Booth. They were both born in 1829 and were married on June 16, 1855. William Booth was ordained to the Methodist ministry on May 27, 1858.[3]

---

[1] Bill J. Leonard, "The Modern Church and Social Action," *Review and Expositor* 85, no. 2 (Spring 1988), 243.

[2] Ibid., 244.

[3] *The Salvation Army Year Book* (London: The General of the Salvation Army, 1990), 32.

William and Catherine began a ministry in East London in 1865. Its name was originally The Christian Revival Association, shortly afterward changed to The Christian Mission. The first headquarters for the ministry was opened at a building on Whitechapel Road in London in 1867. The name Salvation Army was first used in 1878, and William Booth became its first General. The Army's doctrines and principles were adopted the same year.[4]

In 1868 William and Catherine began to publish a magazine entitled *East London Evangelist*. In 1879 the name of the magazine was changed to *The Christian Mission Magazine*, later *The Salvationist*. Catherine Booth designed and sewed the first Salvation Army flag and presented it to a meeting of members and supporters in Coventry in 1878. The Army's doctrines and principles and the "Orders and Regulations" were issued at the same meeting. Brass musical instruments were used in the Army's ministry for the first time that same year.[5]

One Sunday morning in Nottingham, Booth led a group of shabby, ragged, filthy, foul-smelling persons out of the slums into Wesley Chapel and down the aisle to the best seats available. The Chapel's authorities instructed Booth to take his people to less conspicuous benches the next time he brought them to church. But Booth continued to lead every person to the front, as close as possible to Christ. He felt that anyone who took the plunge into human misery for the purpose of extricating the miserable could not afford to be fainthearted in choosing the means. In doing so himself, he rescued many human beings from poverty, vice, and misery.[6] In keeping with this tradition, the objectives of the Salvation Army continue to be the advancement of the Christian religion, the advancement of education, the relief of poverty, and "other charitable objects beneficial to society or the community of mankind as a whole."[7]

Every member of the Salvation Army is required to read, affirm, and sign the "Articles of War: A Soldier's Covenant." The Articles of War begin, "Having accepted Jesus Christ as my Savior and Lord, and desiring to fulfill my membership of His Church on earth as a soldier of the Salvation Army, I now by God's grace enter into a sacred covenant." They go on to state eleven articles of faith. One of the prominent statements in the Articles of War is, "I will be

---

[4]Ibid.
[5]Ibid.
[6]Heinz Vonhoff, *People Who Care* (Philadelphia: Fortress Press, 1960), 227.
[7]*Salvation Army Year Book*, 36-37.

faithful to the purposes for which God raised up The Salvation Army, sharing the good news of Jesus Christ, endeavoring to win others to Him, and in His name caring for the needy and the disadvantaged."[8] From its very beginning the Salvation Army has integrated evangelism and social ministry.

The Volunteers of America

Ballington and Maud Booth came to America to expand the mission enterprise of the Salvation Army. However, there was a disagreement between them and General William Booth, Ballington's father. In 1896 Ballington and Maud established the Volunteers of America. While they used a very strongly regimented organizational structure, they did not use uniforms or ranks in the same way as the Salvation Army. From the beginning they included material assistance in addition to spiritual comfort and guidance as a vital part of their missionary efforts. The mission statement reflects this expanded service concept: "The Volunteers of America is a movement organized for the reaching and uplifting of all people and bringing them to the immediate knowledge and active service of God."[9]

Maud Booth, founder of the Volunteer Prison League, was the first woman ever to visit Sing Sing Prison. She was directly responsible for numerous humanitarian prison reforms. This identification with prison ministries is carried on today by various units of the Volunteers of America.[10]

By the mid-1950s the Volunteers of America had become one of the largest human service providers in America. They presently work in partnership with business, government, churches, and kindred social service agencies in over two hundred communities nationwide. Volunteers of America is one of the primary agencies that has entered into a program designed to "privatize" services formerly provided by the government. Private and church-related agencies can deliver social services at a fraction of what it costs the government to deliver the same services. They are anticipating future expansion of their ministries to include such national issues as day care, literacy, and special programs aimed at youth who are experiencing difficulty with school and may be at high risk of drop-

---

[8]Ibid., 36-37.
[9]*History of the Volunteers of America*, a copy contained in an information package distributed by the Volunteers of America office in Fort Worth, Texas (1987).
[10]Ibid.

ping out. Volunteers of America has also begun to work with youth who are troubled by drug and alcohol abuse.[11]

According to a recent report, the Volunteers of America served 270,283 persons in need of food, clothing, and shelter in 1989. This constitutes about half of their efforts. The Volunteers of America family life program served 133,731 persons. One hundred twenty thousand persons were served by Volunteers of America's health and rehabilitation services. Overall, the Volunteers of America provided social services to 540,566 persons in fiscal year 1988-1989.[12]

Miscellaneous Voluntary Societies

Often born out of spiritual awakenings in England and America, eighteenth- and nineteenth-century benevolent activity by Protestants was best done by voluntary societies. Generally, they were interdenominational and independent bodies formed for particular social, missionary, or benevolent endeavors. Some groups put their emphasis on Christian education and on printing tracts and Bibles. Others confronted some of the moral ills of their day, such as drunkenness, lewdness, gambling, and obscenity.

As denominations became stronger in nineteenth-century America, they organized their own societies to establish hospitals, to perform benevolence activities, and to address serious social issues of their day. One example was the appointment of Joseph Tuckerman in 1826 as minister at large for the Benevolent Fraternity of Churches, a Unitarian society. Tuckerman was described as "an effective social welfare worker, a crusader for his cause, and an influential theorist." Other denominational societies in America focused on education, hospitals, prison reform, temperance, and the abolition of slavery. Protestant leaders helped form the American Temperance Union in 1826, which influenced early American feminism. They also helped form the American Anti-Slavery Society in 1833. This issue divided the three largest Protestant denominations—Methodists, Baptists, and Presbyterians.[13]

American Evangelicals

Two major themes characterize evangelical Christianity in America after the Civil War: perfectionistic theology and postmil-

---

[11]Ibid.
[12]*Volunteers of America 1989 Annual Report* (Metairie, Louisiana: Volunteers of America, Inc., 1989).
[13]Leonard, "The Modern Church and Social Action," 245-247.

lennial eschatology. The perfectionistic theology called Christians to become involved in such issues as poverty, working men's rights, the liquor traffic, slum housing, and racial bitterness. Numerous movements sprang up among evangelical Christians to address one or more of these issues.[14]

One of the greatest names in the evangelical movement was Charles G. Finney. He would not be considered a social revolutionary, but his message encouraged Christians to put their own interests after the needs of others. He encouraged new Christians to express their changed lives through service. Finney felt that revivals could be undermined by insensitivity to the needs to reform society. He stated in his book, *Lectures on Revivals of Religion*, that "revivals are hindered when ministers and churches take wrong ground in regard to any question involving human rights."[15]

Before the Civil War many of Finney's followers were among the staunchest of abolitionists, preaching conversion of sinners and emancipation of slaves. Finney, who held strong antislavery sentiments, became president of Oberlin College and led the school to become the seedbed of radical abolitionism, feminism, and perfectionism. These attitudes grew out of a postmillennial eschatology. Postmillennialism taught that Jesus would return after the church had brought in the millennial kingdom. This belief contributed to a more optimistic interpretation of Christian social action. Christians adhering to this view believed that by winning the lost to Christ, infiltrating society with Christian ideals, and advocating for social change toward a Christian world view, there would be peace on the earth for a thousand years and Jesus would return to a world which had been won to Him.[16]

Toward the end of the nineteenth century many evangelicals became disenchanted with the postmillennial view and turned to premillennialism. Premillennial eschatology stated that the world would get worse and worse; then Jesus would come to set up His kingdom on earth for a thousand years. Satan would be bound, and there would be no evil influence on earth. Jesus would personally rule the earth and bring peace. The primary challenge of premillennialists was to "snatch as many from the burning" as possible before Christ returned.

---

[14]Timothy Smith, *Revivalism and Social Reform* (Gloucester, Mass.: Peter Smith, 1976), 148-177.

[15]Donald W. Dayton, *Discovering an Evangelical Heritage* (San Francisco: Harper and Row, Publishers, 1976), 18.

[16]Ibid.

While premillennialists encouraged Christians to give attention to immediate pressing social needs, they saw no logic in pursuing long-range social reform. This view contributed significantly to what became known as the liberal-fundamentalist controversy. This controversy led to a division between evangelical, soul-saving Christians and reforming social-action Christians—indeed, between evangelical and social Christianity.[17]

The Social Gospel

Around the end of the nineteenth century and the beginning of the twentieth century, a movement began to form out of a coalition of American church groups which was aimed at "Christianizing the social order." It became known as the social gospel movement. Martin Marty stated that the term "social gospel" was probably first used by Charles Brown, an Iowa Congregationalist minister.[18] However, the person who is recognized as the mover and shaper of the social gospel movement was a German Baptist minister, Walter Rauschenbusch. Rauschenbusch was a product of the post-Civil War. He considered himself an evangelical. But as a pastor in the area of New York City known as "Hell's Kitchen," he began to feel that traditional preaching, Sunday School, and revival services were making little difference in the lives of the people in his community. Feeling that in order to make a difference, the gospel must be integrated into the everyday lives of people, he began to preach and teach the social aspects of Christian faith. While he accepted the need for individual conversion, he believed that Christianizing society was the primary business of Christian churches. Christian leaders who had accepted a postmillennial eschatology tended to accept Rauschenbusch's teachings. Evangelical church leaders who had turned to the premillennial view of eschatology tended to reject him and his message.

Bill Leonard stated that the rise of the social gospel came about as a result of numerous influences. One was an attempt to deal with serious social problems that had been exacerbated by the Industrial Revolution. These included slums, labor unrest, urban blight, exploitation of the poor, and inequities of business practices in the industrial cities. A second was a reaction to the capitalistic view of Christianity, which stressed a "trickle-down" approach of

[17]Leonard, "The Modern Church and Social Action," 249.
[18]Martin E. Marty, *Modern American Religion, vol. 1, The Irony of It All, 1893-1919* (Chicago: University of Chicago Press, 1986), 286.

Christians who were blessed by wealth to provide for the poor. This approach allowed for an implicit view that poverty was a result of, if not a punishment for, sin. Thus, all poor persons were first viewed as sinners who were receiving their just desserts. A third reason for the growth of the social gospel was an acceptance of the theology of religious liberalism and social progress. A rift was widening between liberals and conservatives, which was reflected in a social approach versus an individual approach to ministry and evangelism.[19]

Primarily, the social gospel had its greatest acceptance in the industrial cities of the northern United States. The more agrarian southern cities did not experience the same degree of social degradation. Thus, evangelical leaders in the South tended to reject the social gospel along with other liberal theological views regarding social progress. They did, however, embrace some social gospel issues, such as alcoholism and gambling. They often led movements to abolish the open practice of drinking alcoholic beverages and various forms of gambling.

Salvationists and Rescue Missions

In the late nineteenth century and the twentieth century, a major rift appeared among persons working to meet the needs of the poor and oppressed persons. Moberg stated that the question of how to deal with poverty and other interrelated problems divided Christians into two camps. One built a case for evangelism and the conversion of persons as the primary solution. The other emphasized direct social involvement with those systems perceived to be causing the difficulties.[20] This was especially true of programs to help persons who lived in the slum areas of the cities.

Social gospel proponents preached radical social reform because of the oppressive nature of the capitalistic system. The Industrial Revolution had contributed to the formation of large slum areas of every major industrial city. However, they continued to separate the worthy poor from the unworthy poor. For example, Washington Gladden, one of the pioneers of the social gospel movement, chided reform leaders who saw the greed and heartlessness of capitalists and corporations but overlooked the selfish-

---

[19]Bill J. Leonard, "Church and Culture: A Moral Dilemma," *Review and Expositor*, 73, no. 2 (Spring 1976): 145-147.
[20]David O. Moberg, *The Great Reversal* (Philadelphia: J. B. Lippincott Company, 1972), 13.

ness of the poorer classes. He stated that many of the unemployed did not want to work and urged that helpers continue to apply work tests before supplying aid. In contrast, Jane Addams of Hull House rebuked the same group for their fear that the people they aided might not really deserve assistance. Social gospel proponents did not support the Salvation Army because of what they considered careless welfare practices by the Army.[21]

No welfare workers or settlement house workers were more accepting than those involved in the evangelistic welfare movement. These "salvationists" accepted former prisoners, prostitutes, unwed mothers, vagrants, and/or the unemployed with openness and warmth, no matter how much trouble they might have caused. These rescue mission workers felt that given a proper chance, even the most difficult person could be reformed with God's help.[22]

The motivation for accepting and aiding the dispossessed with compassion, optimism, and belief in the worth of every person came from the nature of the evangelistic welfare movement workers' religious experience and teaching. This teaching, centered on godly love, was expressed practically, sacrificially, sensitively, and helpfully. Their presence in the slums familiarized them with the needs and the oppressive nature of the urban environment. The needs were too vast for these rescue mission workers to become preoccupied with one problem. They embraced disadvantaged persons of all types, including African-Americans, Orientals, and the "new" immigrants. These were the classes of people the social gospelers and the leaders of the larger progressive movements appear to have neglected.[23]

Denominational Models

All contemporary Christian denominations in America express some sense of the integration of beliefs and social ministry. These may be broken down into four models. One model assumes that beliefs are the most essential of the two dimensions and that social ministry is a by-product rather than the focus of faith. Groups who adopt this model are usually theologically and socially conservative in their orientation. They feel that the more faithful

---

[21]Norris Magnuson, *Salvation in the Slums: Evangelical Social Work 1865-1920* (Grand Rapids: Baker Book House, 1977), xvi-xvii.
[22]Ibid., xviii.
[23]Ibid.

members are to the belief system, the more concerned they will be about the poor and needy.

The second model assumes that social ministry is more important than the belief system and that effective social ministries will enhance people's faith. These "liberal" denominations feel that the more churches and individual churchgoers are involved in social and community issues related to the needs of the poor, needy, and powerless, the more their faith will grow.

A third view is that beliefs and social ministry are of equal importance. In this "dualistic" view, the twin goals of growth in faith and growth in service are given equal attention by the denomination. The denomination does not attempt to forge a linkage between faith and social ministry; however, its leaders expect individual members and congregations to forge one.

The fourth model is an integrated one which assumes that the two are equally important and inseparable. According to this "holistic" view, beliefs and social ministry are given equal emphasis because they reinforce and support each other. Faith is not viable if it is not expressed in concern for persons in need, and social concern is not sensible if it is not accompanied by faith.[24]

The denominations that tend to follow model 1 are the Southern Baptists, the Churches of Christ, and the Church of the Nazarene, along with a group of largely independent evangelical and Holiness churches. Model 2 churches would include the Episcopal Church, the United Church of Christ, and the Presbyterian Church (USA). Moderate Protestant churches would adapt more readily to models 3 and 4. They include the United Methodists, the American Lutherans, and the American Baptists. Roman Catholics and Black Protestants tend to have representations from several models. There is a great deal of variation among each of the denominations and groups just listed above. It is very difficult to generalize about any of these groups.

The following discussion is intended to address representative models rather than to provide a comprehensive discussion. We will begin with brief discussions of the more liberal churches and end with the conservative ones.

The Episcopal Church

Over the years the Episcopal Church has supported numerous social ministry programs and institutions. For example, in

---

[24]James D. Davidson, Lincoln C. Johnson, and Alan K. Mock, eds., *Faith and Social Ministry* (Chicago: Loyola University Press, 1990), 11-12.

almost every major city there are Episcopal hospitals. Local parishes are generally counted upon to support local charities and relief efforts. However, in recent years, interest and concern for social issues appears to be waning in the Episcopal Church. The degree to which members engage in social ministries tends to be the result of how pressing an issue is locally, rather than a general concern for the poor, needy, and powerless in general. One Episcopal writer has said, "Parish social ministry increasingly involves people willing to give money to relief efforts, but not about to challenge governmental policy, which in many instances is responsible for the particular social concern to which the ministry is addressed."[25]

The Presbyterian Church (USA)

According to Hargrove and Wilbanks, the Presbyterian Church regards social ministry as an integral part of its life and mission. In addition to being a vital element in the Christian life of individual members, social ministry is also a responsibility of the corporate bodies of congregations, presbyteries, synods, and the General Assembly. Presbyterian theological heritage has produced advocates of systemic change and leaders who have engaged the church in compassionate service. For example, the Presbyterian General Assembly led all other denominations in advocating housing, food, education, and health services for Mexican and Central American immigrants. It also called upon the United States government to change the immigration laws.[26]

Support for social ministry by Presbyterians generally has an ecumenical orientation. In general, support for a strong public and corporate social ministry is greatest among those who are full-time servants. Those who favor private acts of charity are generally found among the rank and file. The corporate body of the Presbyterian Church is well organized to provide study materials and other forms of communication, which have a significant impact on local congregations and individual members.[27] This has led to a fairly comprehensive scope of social ministry programs sponsored by the church. In addition to vigorous social action programs for systemic

---

[25]Edward Rodman, "Faith and Social Ministry: A View of the Episcopal Church," *Faith and Social Ministry*, ed. Davidson and others (Chicago: Loyola University Press, 1990), 30-33.

[26]Barbara Hargrove and Dana Wilbanks, "Faith and Social Ministry in the Presbyterian Church (USA)," *Faith and Social Ministry*, ed. Davidson and others (Chicago: Loyola University, 1990), 63.

[27]Ibid., 69.

CHRISTIAN SOCIAL MINISTRY

change, these include such programs and services as shelters for homeless persons, hospitals, children's homes, community centers, and various programs for the hungry and otherwise destitute.

United Church of Christ

Growing out of a Puritan and Congregational heritage in New England, the United Church of Christ has a rich history of social ministries. In the colonial days of New England, the churches were generally an integral part of every community. As such, one writer commented that "There have scarcely ever been communities where the poor and needy were more carefully, though frugally, looked after than obtained in the New England towns. . . . In these town meetings church people have always taken an active part in behalf of justice and well-being. . . . The church had for its mission the cure of injustice and the lifting of the level of the whole of life."[28]

For congregants in the United Church of Christ, faith and social ministry are not synonymous; they are woven into the very fabric of the denomination. According to Frederick Trost, the term social ministry in the United Church of Christ is understood to be any form of service offered in grateful response to "the Word made flesh," God with us in the world. "It is, in a sense, conformity to Christ; being present to brothers and sisters in the name of Christ. It is celebrated in our liturgies. It is sung in our hymns. It is attempting to live out the meaning of our creeds."[29]

The strength of a denomination's commitment to social ministry can be seen in the allocation of its resources. In the 1990-1991 budget proposal, 19.5 percent was devoted to church development and evangelism. The third highest percentage, 16.7 percent, went to social concerns. This included projects focusing on peace, arms control, economic justice, racism, sexism, toxic waste disposal, advocacy for people in poverty, voting rights, human rights divestment, and the social responsibility of corporations.

Methodists

John and Charles Wesley, the founders of Methodism in England, also had a dynamic impact on American evangelicalism.

---

[28]G. C. Atkins and F. L. Fagley, *History of American Congregationalism* (Boston: Pilgrim Press, 1942), 248.

[29]Frederick R. Trost, "The Meaning of 'Faith' and the Commitment to 'Social Ministry' in the United Church of Christ," *Faith and Social Ministry*, ed. Davidson and others (Chicago: Loyola University Press, 1990), 35-40.

Even today they are widely known, for their contributions went beyond the form of worship and the evangelistic efforts of congregations. However, they were very much involved in social ministries. On October 14, 1735, John and Charles sailed from England to Savannah, Georgia, where they were to serve in the colony established by Oglethorpe. They were to administer a "trust for the poor" while working toward "the conversion of slaves."[30] George Whitefield succeeded the Wesleys and, in 1738, established the first Methodist children's home, Bethesda Orphan's Asylum. Thirty years after its founding it was destroyed by fire. He raised the money for his philanthropic activities throughout the colonies as well as in England and Scotland.[31]

Methodists, along with other evangelical denominations, were famous for circuit-riding pastors during the frontier days of America. Social ministry played a large part in the work of the circuit riders. Many of them learned as much as they could about the simple medical practices of their day. These ministers helped many persons who did not have access to doctors. The circuit riders also took up offerings to help destitute persons, and sometimes whole communities. Even after Methodist preachers were able to settle down and pastor larger, more stable congregations, their social ministry continued and often increased with intensity.[32]

Over the years Methodists have been at the forefront in developing social service institutions such as schools, hospitals, children's homes, and homes for older persons. The oldest Methodist institution still in existence is the Warren A. Candler Memorial Hospital in Savannah, Georgia. One of the oldest homes for the aged is the New York Methodist Church Home, which dates back to 1850.[33]

Methodist researchers Philip Amerson and Earl Brewer state that there has been a shift among the laity regarding its chief aim. The mission statement of the church reads, "The aim of mission is to release in both individual and society the redemptive power of God disclosed in Jesus Christ, so that all human life may be made whole." In 1958, 23.8 percent of the laity agreed with this statement. At the same time most of the clergy agreed with it. In 1980, 53.9 per-

---

[30]Haskel M. Miller, *Compassion and Community* (New York: Association Press, 1961), 77-78.

[31]Eric M. North, *Early Methodist Philanthropy* (New York: Methodist Book Concern, 1914), 89.

[32]Wade Crawford Barclay, ed., *History of Methodist Missions: Early American Methodism, 1769-1844 in Two Volumes* (New York: The Board of Missions and Church Extension of the Methodist Church, 1950), vol. 2, *To Reform the Nation*, 9.

[33]Miller, *Compassion and Community*, 78-79.

cent of the laity agreed with the statement, while 81 percent of the clergy stated that they agreed with it.[34]

Brewer and Jackson studied the attitudes of Methodists regarding six major social ministry issues: lack of belief in God as sustainer of daily life; starvation and poverty; discrimination, exploitation, or oppression based on race, sex, age, economic class, religion, and ethnic or national rights; lack of a sense of holiness; wars and arms races; and misuse of earth's resources. The results indicated that Methodists felt strongest about lack of belief in God as sustainer of daily life. Less than one point below was concern for starving and poverty-based persons. Discrimination, exploitation, and oppression ranked third.

Respondents were asked to describe what should be done to remedy the problems. The first strategy was to proclaim God's love as manifested in Jesus Christ to all, with an invitation to become disciples. The second strategy was to develop stewardship beliefs and practices that preserve God's earth, feed the hungry, and share the earth's resources with all people. The third strategy was to work for a world without discrimination, exploitation, and oppression. The fourth strategy was to join the poor in struggles for survival and/or economic and social justice.[35]

American Lutheranism

Although organized Lutheran work developed more slowly than that of the Methodists and Baptists and others, some significant events did take place under the leadership of Dr. W. A. Passavant. His first accomplishment was the establishment of a hospital in Pittsburgh in 1849. He introduced the Protestant Order of Deaconesses into America by bringing a group of Lutheran sisters from Kaiserswerth. Soon other denominations were organizing similar groups.[36]

According to Ross Scherer, the primary Lutheran approach to defining the relationship of the Christian to society has been the "doctrine of the two kingdoms," which was institutionalized by the church in the eighteenth century. Within the church, ideally, the Word of God is to be followed, whereas in society, the coercion of law was used by the state. The traditional position of Lutherans has

---

[34]Philip A. Amerson and Earl D. C. Brewer, "Faith and Social Ministry: United Methodism," in *Faith and Social Ministry*, ed. Davidson and others (Chicago: Loyola University Press, 1990), 88-89.
[35]Ibid.
[36]Miller, *Compassion and Community*, 79.

been that a person is not saved by works, but works are expected to follow conversion as fruits of faith and forgiveness by God. In recent years the major Lutheran groups (Lutheran Church in America; American Lutheran Church; and Lutheran Church, Missouri Synod) have taken public stands on the following issues:

> Church and state, religious liberty, civil disobedience, peace and human rights, environment, ecology, farm management, public schools and religion, tuition tax credits, church and human welfare, the aged, socioeconomic justice, poverty and tax policies, capital punishment and crime, the American Indian, racism, apartheid, sexism, abortion, marriage and the family, human sexuality, pornography, gambling, nuclear disarmament, war, conscientious objection, medical technology and terminal illness, death and dying.[37]

American Baptist Churches

The American Baptist churches share a rich heritage of social involvement with most other Baptist groups. In fact, the American Baptist denomination (originally known as Northern Baptists) came into being as a result of their concern for relating faith to social responsibility. Baptists of the Northern part of the United States were very involved in the antislavery movement. This issue eventually led to the division of Baptists in America between North and South.

Southern Baptists had great difficulty in accepting Walter Rauschenbusch and the social gospel. His teachings more heartily influenced American Baptists. In both home and foreign missions, the social emphasis has been an integral part of the faith and works of American Baptists.

In more recent years (1984-1990), the American Baptist Churches in the U.S.A. embarked upon a major six-year emphasis which spoke to the issue of integrating faith and social ministry. This program emphasized nine "marks" of a caring and growing church: personal witness, social witness, discipleship, leadership, congregational growth, service, stewardship, cooperation, and identity. According to Jones, "The emphasis was on a sense of wholeness which leads to personal, congregational, missional, edu-

---

[37]Ross P. Scherer, "Faith and Social Ministry in American Lutheranism," *Faith and Social Ministry,* ed. Davidson and others (Chicago: Loyola University Press, 1990), 102-106.

cational growth resulting from engaging in caring concern for others and the needs of the world."[38]

The Holiness Churches

The American Holiness movement was, in its earliest inception, a social reform movement. Some have thought that a primary factor in the development of the Holiness movement was a reaction to the social gospel. This was not the case. In fact, each of the movements gave rise to similar theological positions. Slavery was one of the first social issues to catch the attention of the holiness proponents. Most were abolitionists. Oberlin College, Wesleyan Methodists, and Free Methodists all worked at both the structural and individual levels for the abolishment of slavery.[39]

Feminism was also a part of the early holiness movement. Oberlin College, for example, was the first college in America to accept women students. The first women's rights convention was held in a Wesleyan Methodist church. Women were allowed to function in every aspect of the churches, including serving as pastors, evangelists, missionaries, and educators.[40]

In the middle of the twentieth century, holiness groups, including the Church of the Nazarene, became more involved in mainstream Protestantism as they became more affluent. They began to turn from their early emphasis upon the poor, the dispossessed, and the oppressed. Part of the reason had to do with a distrust of the social activism of the more liberal churches. Another part involved a shift in theological emphasis from loving and doing to faith and acceptance.

There are some positive signs suggesting a return to their roots. The Church of the Nazarene is now taking steps to return to the city from which it was born. The denomination has launched a new program entitled "Thrust to the Cities." They will attempt to locate new churches within the major inner cities by developing ministries among minority groups. In other words, they are returning to the Holiness emphasis upon reaching the socially disinher-

---

[38]Richard M. Jones, "Faith and Social Ministry: American Baptist Views," *Faith and Social Ministry*, ed. Davidson and others (Chicago: Loyola University Press, 1990), 127-129.

[39]Donald W. Dayton, "The Holiness Churches: A Significant Ethical Tradition," *The Christian Century* (26 February 1975), 197-201.

[40]Ibid.

ited, the poor, the outcasts, the "rejects." For such persons the movement began in the first place.[41]

African-American Churches

The earliest African-American churches emphasized the importance of political freedom, social justice, and religious liberty. The central problem of African-American churches during their formative years was slavery, and their ministries reflected that fact. One problem the churches faced was divorce and remarriage. This problem was exacerbated by the fact that slave families were often split up and sold to different plantation owners. Therefore, the church found it necessary to accommodate divorce and remarriage. This factor was not openly accepted by the Anglo-American church leaders. Another problem had to do with closed communion; Anglo-American churches would not take communion to the fields, where the slaves were required to work on Sunday.[42]

Racism was not isolated to the southern churches. Along with black Methodists and Episcopalians, black Baptists were victims of segregation in the slave galleries of northern churches. In New York City, the Abyssinian Baptist Church, the African Methodist Episcopal Church, and the African Methodist Episcopal Zion Church were formed as a protest of this racist behavior on the part of northern churches.[43]

The history of African-American churches, especially the African-American Baptist churches, is that of organizational and institutional approaches to social ministry. This ministry is expressed in efforts for social change, racial uplift, home missions, and education. One of the most famous persons in recent American history, Martin Luther King, Jr., an African-American National Baptist pastor, led a fight for racial justice. His memory continues to inspire African-Americans, as well as people of all races, to press on toward social justice for all people.

The integration of faith and social ministry in dynamic interaction leads to a practical interpretation of the message of Christ and demands radical action in order for a Christian to live out that principle. Rev. T. J. Jemison, who was elected president of the

---

[41]Michael K. Roberts, "Nazarenes and Social Ministry: A Holiness Tradition," *Faith and Social Ministry*, ed. Davidson and others (Chicago: Loyola University Press, 1990), 165-169.

[42]Cheryl Townsend Gilkes, "'Until My Change Comes': In the African-American Baptist Tradition," *Faith and Social Ministry*, ed. Davidson and others (Chicago: Loyola University Press, 1990), 185.

[43]Ibid., 182.

National Baptist Convention in 1983, suggested that rather than working with the "underprivileged," the church should be involved in "a re-visioning or redefining of 'privilege'." Underprivileged is an inoperative term for describing persons who are essentially without the privileges or benefits of the system. It is the task of the church to minister to those who are not even underprivileged, but unprivileged.[44]

Roman Catholic

Historically the Roman Catholic Church has, through its numerous orders, emphasized institutional ministries. It has never been bashful about being involved with government, particularly when there was an issue of social concern. Over the years, according to Neal, the Catholic Church has proceeded through a number of paradigm shifts. She stated that the major paradigm shift in the past four decades, characterizing the relationship of faith and social ministry in the Catholic Church, has been to a new focus on social ministry. The thrust of this shift is in preparing clergy and laity for "a special option for the poor as a guide to ministry and expression of faith." The stimulus for this emphasis has come from the Medellin Conference of the Latin American church in 1967.[45]

Over the years, the Catholic Church has defined ministry in different ways. Today, *ministry* refers to what the people are doing to fulfill this newly defined mission. It involves social action activities such as community building and transforming, which are integrated into parish life and push toward societal transformation. This transformation is perceived as mandated by the gospel with the intention that the world's resources become available to all people.[46]

Southern Baptist Convention

Southern Baptists are the largest group of non-Catholic Christians in America. They are also considered the most theologically conservative of the major denominations. The integration of faith and social ministry by Southern Baptists begins with what E. Y. Mullins called "soul competency." Jere Allen quoted him as saying that "The idea of the soul's competency embraces the social as well as the individual aspect of religion." For Mullins, social con-

---

[44]Ibid., 192-197.

[45]Marie Augusta Neal, "Faith and Social Ministry: A Catholic Perspective," *Faith and Social Ministry*, ed. Davidson and others (Chicago: Loyola University Press, 1990), 205.

[46]Ibid., 212-217.

sciousness and social concern spontaneously arise from regeneration. For Southern Baptists, social ministry evolves from faith.

Most Southern Baptist ministers, however, are somewhat selective in the social action issues that they will allow to attract their attention. They will not usually accept the broad social action agenda of the other major denominations. Instead, they choose to focus their attention on certain selected areas such as gambling, pornography, and alcohol abuse.[47]

Persons outside the Southern Baptist Convention may find it difficult, if not contradictory, to believe that Southern Baptists have a very strong emphasis on social ministry. Perhaps this is due to the narrow focus of Southern Baptist leaders on social action. It may also be due to the fact that most discussions at denominational gatherings are about evangelism, missions, and how to explain the Bible. In recent years Southern Baptists have been severely divided over whether to use the word "inerrant" in referring to the Bible, as opposed to simply saying that the Bible is the inspired Word of God.

While the controversy over the Bible has been going on, however, local congregations, associations, state conventions, and various boards and agencies of the denomination have been continuing to plan and implement a wide array of social ministry programs. At the denominational level, the Home Mission Board has a division of ministry which is on equal footing with evangelism, church extension, services and planning. Over three hundred missionaries are currently appointed for the purpose of helping local congregations, associations, and state conventions to plan and implement programs of social ministry. Ministry programs are also considered to be an integral part of foreign mission work and receive significant emphasis by the Southern Baptist Foreign Mission Board.

One of the largest publishing companies in the United States is the Southern Baptist Sunday School Board. In addition to publishing Bibles, books, and periodicals, the Sunday School Board has a division that produces support materials and programs for ministries with couples, families, single adults, and senior adults.

Southern Baptists support hospitals, children's homes, and homes for the aged in almost every section of the United States. In almost every major city and in some rural areas, Southern Baptists have organized ministries to poverty-bound persons in the inner cities. These ministries include such programs as literacy, adult basic

---

[47]William Jere Allen, "Faith, Social Ministry, and Linkage Between the Two in the Southern Baptist Convention," *Faith and Social Action*, ed. Davidson and others (Chicago: Loyola University Press, 1990), 146-148.

education, English as a second language, parenting and guidance programs, problem pregnancy counseling, hospice ministries, tutoring, well-child clinics, emergency food and clothing distribution, hunger relief, drug and alcohol counseling, and released offender reentry, as well as ministry with the hearing impaired, the sight impaired, the mentally impaired, and the physically handicapped.

The Southern Baptist agency that has primary responsibility for program development in Christian social ministries is the Home Mission Board. From its beginning, the Home Mission Board has been responsible for ministry with the disadvantaged. The first major project supported by the Home Mission Board was the Seamen's Institute in Jacksonville, Florida, which began in 1919. During that same year a sanatorium was opened in El Paso, Texas. In 1927 a rescue mission (now the Clovis Brantley Baptist Center) was opened in New Orleans, Louisiana. This was followed by the opening of the Sellers Baptist Home and Adoption Center, also in New Orleans, in 1937.

The Home Mission Board began a ministry to migrant workers in 1947, which was followed by the initiation of community centers during the 1950s and 1960s. These centers were fashioned after settlement house programs. During the 1960s the program of ministry support was broadened to include literacy missions, church weekday ministries, and disaster relief. In 1966, the Department of Christian Social Ministries was established under the leadership of Paul Adkins, and was recognized as an official program of the Southern Baptist Convention.[48]

Currently the Christian Social Ministries Department is entitled the Church and Community Ministries Department (CCM). It is housed in the Mission Ministries Division of the Ministries Section of the Home Mission Board. The Church and Community Ministries Department has responsibility for developing programs and support materials for institutional ministries, criminal justice and substance abuse, literacy missions, and ministries with single and senior adults, families, and disabled persons.

Seminary Education for Social Ministries

There appears to be a renewed interest in theological education for social ministry among mainline denominational seminaries. In 1987 the Lilly Endowment's Religion Division funded a

---

[48]Ronald Loftis, *Church and Community Ministries Director's Manual* (Atlanta: Home Mission Board, 1987), preface.

Symposium on Theological Education for Socially Responsible Ministry. The symposium was held in Washington, D.C., under the leadership of the Social Education staff of the Presbyterian Program Agency. Participants in the symposium represented Lutherans, United Methodists, Presbyterians, the United Church of Christ, the Disciples of Christ, and the Episcopal Church. Notably absent from the invitation list were Southern Baptists and other evangelical seminary professors.[49]

An impressive group of contributors was invited to present papers at the symposium. They were Terence R. Anderson, Vancouver School of Theology; James D. Beumler, Princeton University; Jacquelyn Grant, Interdenominational Theological Center, Atlanta, Georgia; Dieter T. Hessel, director of the Presbyterian Church (USA) Committee on Social Witness Policy; Karen Lebacqz, Pacific School of Religion; James C. Logan, Wesley Theological Seminary; Larry L. Rasmussen, Union Theological Seminary, New York City; and Ronald H. Stone, Pittsburgh Theological Seminary.

Karen Lebacqz summed up the symposium's composite definition of social ministry: Socially responsible ministry involves a "radical critique" of society. It is Christian practice that "envisions the whole," placing ministry in the context of large social trends. There is no neutral ministry. All ministry is socially responsive in some way. Socially responsible ministry requires social analysis and consciousness of the ethos in which we live. It features praxis or struggle for liberation of the oppressed. It requires critical awareness of tendencies that derive from our own social location. Socially responsible ministry participates in the unified mission of the church. Socially responsive ministry is oriented to doing justice, making peace, and caring for creation. Socially responsive ministry requires "solidarity"—loyalty to disregarded people, not ideological causes.[50]

None of the seminaries included in the symposium have a specific program for training ministers in social work or social ministry. Those who convened the symposium also studied the curricula of a number of theological seminaries accredited by the Association of Theological Schools. In addition to the seminaries and schools represented by the presenters at the symposium, Eastern Baptist Theological Seminary, Virginia Theological Seminary,

---

[49]Dieter T. Hessel, ed., *Theological Education for Social Ministry* (New York: Pilgrim Press, 1988), ix.
[50]Ibid., 2.

and Luther Northwestern Seminary were chosen "to represent a better range of Protestant theological education."[51]

Southern Baptists are unique in providing seminary training for persons preparing for a career in social ministry. Most denominationally related seminaries have courses in social ethics and in practical theology. These courses are most often related to social concerns in the church and the larger community. However, curricula and degrees leading to the specialized practice of social ministries in the church and denomination are almost exclusively the domain of Southern Baptist seminaries. This is not a recent phenomenon. As early as 1897, the Southern Baptist Theological Seminary in Louisville, Kentucky, began offering courses in Christian sociology for divinity students. These courses reflected the rising influence of the social gospel and were strongly oriented in social ministry. The professors who taught these courses included such noted theologians as E. C. Dargan, C. S. Gardner, and J. B. Weatherspoon.

In 1907 the Woman's Missionary Union Training School for Christian Workers was founded and located adjacent to the Southern Baptist Theological Seminary. This school began offering training in professional social work in 1912 under the leadership of Maud Reynolds McClure. In order for students to have a social service center in which to acquire professional experience, she simultaneously led in establishing the Training School Settlement House. To some degree the settlement house was modeled after Jane Addam's Hull House. This program has been developed to become the Carver School of Church Social Work of the Southern Baptist Theological Seminary (along with the School of Theology, School of Religious Education, and School of Church Music). It is fully accredited to offer the Master of Social Work degree by the Council on Social Work Education.[52] The Carver School of Church Social Work is the only program in a theological seminary to have ever been accredited by the Council on Social Work Education.

Southwestern Baptist Theological Seminary in Fort Worth, Texas, began offering courses in Christian sociology in 1910. At the same time, Woman's Missionary Union Training School in Fort Worth was offering courses in church social work. In 1915 the Woman's Missionary Union Training School was merged with the semi-

---

[51]James D. Beumler, "Tradition and Change: Curricular Trends in the Recent History of Theological Education," *Theological Education for Social Ministry,* ed. Hessel (New York: The Pilgrim Press, 1988), 148-149.

[52]C. Anne Davis, "History of the Carver School of Church Social Work," *Review and Expositor,* 85, no. 2 (Spring 1988), 209-211.

nary to form the School of Religious Education. J. M. Price became the first dean and insisted that courses in church social work be included in the seminary's curriculum—among the first professional social work courses to be offered in a theological seminary.

Professional social work education for persons preparing for social ministry is offered in two ways at Southwestern Seminary. One approach is to earn a Master of Arts degree in church social services at the seminary. The curriculum includes an integration of classical theological disciplines, church administration and other courses in religious education, and a social work curriculum that parallels a Council on Social Work Education approved master's degree. The second approach is to study the classical theological disciplines, church administration, and religious education courses and to enroll in a master's degree program in a CSWE-accredited graduate school of social work. Upon completion of the student's degree in social work from the university, Southwestern Seminary will then award the Master of Arts degree in church social services. Students earn two professional master's degrees, and they are thus equipped to practice in both church and secular social work agencies. Southwestern Seminary also offers a doctoral degree in social work for persons preparing for advanced church-related social work practice.

New Orleans Baptist Theological Seminary also has a plan allowing students to earn the Master of Arts in Christian Education and the Master of Social Work simultaneously. Students in this program study social work primarily with the graduate schools of social work at Tulane University and Louisiana State University. Garrett Theological Seminary (Methodist), located adjacent to Northwestern University, and Presbyterian School of Christian Education in Richmond, Virginia, have similar relationships with graduate schools of social work in or near their localities.

Summary and Conclusions

Some contemporary ministry models discussed in this chapter are primarily institutional. Others are congregational. Some of the churches and organizations provide extensive help to individual Christians, encouraging them to engage in social ministries. Others provide a general, more philosophical type of emphasis with little direct encouragement for individual Christians to help the poor, needy, and disenfranchised.

A number of the "mainline" denominations express social ministry by engaging in systemic change at the macrosystem level.

These tend to be more moderate and liberal theologically. The more theologically conservative denominations often stress individual and congregational approaches to dealing with human need. These conservative groups are generally selective in the type of social action issues they endorse.

Controversy over whether or not to classify some persons as worthy and others as unworthy continues to be an issue. Salvationists have generally been the most accepting and the least judgmental regarding the worthiness of all persons to receive help.

There appears to be a renewed interest in theological education for social ministry in the seminaries accredited by the Association of Theological Schools. Seminaries sponsored by the Southern Baptist Convention appear to be taking the lead in training ministers for professional-level social ministry. The Southern Baptist Convention seems to be placing direct ministries to persons with human needs on an even par with its other major efforts. Southern Baptists are trying to integrate evangelism and social ministry as a mission strategy for the twenty-first century.

Exercises for Review and Examination

1. Describe and compare the Puritans' and the Quakers' approaches to social ministry.

2. What two major themes shaped the American evangelical approach to social ministry? Please list and briefly define each.

3. Choose one of the American denominations and discuss one issue related to integrating faith and social ministry that is unique to that denomination.

4. Briefly discuss theological education for social ministry in North America.

5. List and describe the four approaches modern denominations take to integrating faith and social ministry.

Chapter Three

Biblical Foundations for Christian Social Ministries

Goals: A study of this chapter should enable the social minister to understand . . .

1. how the Old Testament concepts of righteousness, justice, mercy, and love form a foundation for social ministry.
2. how the New Testament demonstration of love establishes social ministry as a primary function of every Christian.

Objectives: The minister . . .

1. discusses the qualities of an incarnational social minister.
2. delineates a rationale for social ministry in the church based upon Old and New Testament concepts.
3. applies the New Testament concept of *agape* love to the work of the social minister.

As we have seen, history has provided contemporary believers a sense of continuity with Christians in the past in an attempt to establish foundations for Christian social ministries. Part of this tradition is based on our understanding of the Judeo-Christian ethic. In this chapter we will examine the Scriptures to delineate Old Testament and New Testament foundations for the delivery of social services by Christian churches. We will also review the practice of Christian social ministry by persons called of God to be the incarnation of His will.

The search for a biblical basis for social ministry is not like hunting for some obscure proof-text or for the proverbial needle in the haystack. Joel Gregory suggested that often the approach persons take in discussing a biblical social ministry would suggest that the Bible is about something other than ministry, with a few verses here and there about concern for persons in their physical, emotional, and financial deprivation. "On the contrary," he has said, "anywhere you punch the Bible it reveals sensitivity to ministry with persons."[1]

Four concepts consistently appear in the Old Testament, forming the Old Testament foundation for social ministry. They are righteousness, justice, mercy, and love. Building upon these concepts from the Old Testament, the New Testament foundational concepts are love and grace. In this chapter we will attempt to search out the meanings of these concepts as they relate to social ministry.

Old Testament Foundations

As persons encounter God they are struck by the knowledge that a relationship with God is distinctly personal. However, this relationship is not a purely private matter. God, who reveals Himself in the Bible, is concerned with the totality of every person's well-being. One's encounter with God inevitably has an effect upon other relationships and the performance of the Christian's roles in society. Thus the Christian will hold a prominent place for the needs of other persons in his or her world.[2]

The Bible deals not only with humanity's primary relationship with God, but with all human relationships. The biblical account begins with an emphasis upon God's creation of all things and humanity's relationship with them (Gen. 1:1—2:20). Immediately there is a social element injected as woman is created and the social institution of marriage is initiated (Gen. 2:21-25).

Social deviance becomes a reality as sin leads to murder, lying, cheating, adultery, envy, and disrespect for God Himself. God takes the initiative to form laws to deal with these social ills. Covenants are made and kept by God but broken by human beings. The whole Bible is the story of the drama of God's redemptive

---

[1]Joel Gregory, "A Biblical Theology of Ministry," an address delivered to a Ministries Evangelism Workshop sponsored by the Baptist General Convention of Texas, Dallas, Texas, September 1977.

[2]T. B. Maston, "Biblical Basis for Social Concern," *Southwestern Journal of Theology* (April, 1965), 5.

actions among His creation. The first five books deal with the beginning of humanity and the formulation of rules guiding the relationships with God and other humans. The prophets often called attention to the basic social responsibilities and God's will regarding them.

Righteousness

In the Hebrew language the word *righteous* is constructed on the stem *sadaq*. This concept carries with it the idea of conforming to a norm. The Old Testament pictures God as the righteous one (Ps. 4:1; 7:9; Isa. 45:21). All of his actions are righteous (Judg. 5:11; Ps. 71:24; Jer. 12:1). Since He is the source of righteousness, all that He does is in harmony with His character. Every one of God's decrees and laws express his righteous nature (Deut. 4:8; Ps. 119:7, 62, 75, 106, 138, 160, 164, 172).[3]

Christian people are said to be righteous when their behavior approximates that of the moral and ethical norm established in the revealed Word of God—the actions, decrees, and laws of God. To be righteous is to concern oneself with issues about which God is concerned—including, among other things, a sense of responsibility for nature. Everything God created has meaning and purpose and exists in a delicate balance which has been intricately interfaced according to the mind and will of the creator.

Another norm for Christians is a life-style that radiates moral and ethical purity. Evangelical Christians who adhere to a perfectionistic theology emphasize this form of righteousness. This perfectionism is often expressed in rigid moral codes that narrowly define acceptable and unacceptable behavior. Such Christians stress a disciplined life of sinless perfection. Lives in accord with God's moral norm are commendable. God, however, is just as interested in what a person does about a neighbor in need as He is in whether the person drinks, uses tobacco, reads the Bible, or attends church. Another form of perfectionism has to do with doctrinal purity. While doctrinal purity is important, giving mental assent to a set of beliefs and moral codes is not as important to God as meeting the needs of human beings who are poor, sick, disturbed, and disenfranchised (1 Sam. 15:22).

Righteousness is not just an abstract set of moral principles but a behavioral outcome in harmony with one's obligations to

---

[3]Lawrence Richards, *Expository Dictionary of Bible Words* (Grand Rapids: Zondervan Publishing House, 1985), 418.

God. To live a life characterized by righteousness requires one to treat all persons in the same way God would treat them. When persons are thirsty, Christians should offer them a drink of cool water. If persons are hungry, Christians should share food. If they need shelter, Christians should provide it if possible. When persons are unjustly victimized by laws, rules, regulations, or practices, Christians should become involved in changing the system (see the Book of Amos).

In the Old Testament God is portrayed as acting righteously as judge and as Savior. All persons will be judged according to God's *righteousness* (Ps. 9:8; 45:7; 96:13; 98:9). The criteria for this judgment are spelled out in numerous ways in the Old and New Testaments. God hates wickedness. The judgment of a wicked person will include how he has treated the poor, the weak, and the needy. God's judgment is an expression of His intrinsic righteousness. The *righteous* God is also the Savior and Deliverer (Ps. 31:1; 119:40; Isa. 45:21). Only by His righteous actions toward frail humanity could anyone ever be saved. While His judgment will be carried out with absolute justice, His deliverance will be administered by absolute grace for those who trust in Him.[4] Only God can accomplish such a magnificent feat. Social ministers who follow Christ will become the incarnation of His righteousness. God has all power and wisdom; however, He chooses to use human beings as His resources for fulfilling His righteousness. Although the righteousness of persons cannot measure up to the righteousness of God, the Old Testament speaks freely of righteous people (Gen. 6:9; Job 1:1; Ps. 143:2).

There are a number of ways in which the righteousness of human beings is spoken of in the Old Testament. (1) In some passages, human beings are compared with each other. Some are said to be righteous, while others are referred to as unrighteous. One example occurs in Saul's comparison of himself with David (1 Sam. 24:17). (2) When human behavior is characterized by conformity to God's will, it is said to be righteous (Deut. 6:25). (3) The acts of praising, adoring, and serving God are other ways the terms are used with reference to people (Ps. 33:1; 64:10; 140:13; Mal. 3:18). (4) Living a righteous life resulting in multiplied blessings (Ps. 5:12) is another way the term is used. This righteous life is said to bring a sense of being upheld (Ps. 37:17). A righteous life is a flourishing one (Ps. 92:12). One who lives a righteous life will be remembered

---

[4]Ibid.

(Ps. 112:6). Although the righteous may have troubles, God will help them and they will not be forsaken (Ps. 34:19; 37:25; 55:22). (5) The writers of the Old Testament believed that the *righteous* have a better basis for appealing to God (2 Sam. 22:21, 25; Ps. 7:8; 17:1; 18:20,24; 119:121).[5]

Justice

Over four hundred times in the Old Testament, the Hebrew word *mispat* is translated "justice" or "just." When *mispat* is translated "just" it is in the context of "doing what is just." The root *sapat* refers to all functions of government. *Mispat*, in essence, has to do with one's rights and duties under the law.

Sadaq, the Hebrew word most often translated "righteous," is the root for a number of words that are also translated "just" and "justice." These carry the idea of moral and ethical norms. For example, actions that are in harmony with the norm are just, and those which are not are unjust. This Old Testament Hebrew root and its derivatives are also translated "right" and "righteous."[6] Ultimately, our understanding of justice, like that of righteousness, has its source in the Giver of the law. Deuteronomy 32:4 says, "He is the Rock, his works are perfect, and all his ways are just. A faithful God who does no wrong, upright and just is he." Justice is rooted in the very nature of God, and His nature is the true sample. All His behaviors are just and right, whether we can understand them or not.[7] Richards stated that often the prophets called Israel back to a just life-style. The Hebrew people drifted into the practice of injustice, often while practicing the forms of their religion very meticulously. They questioned why God would be allowing bad things to happen to them while they had been so faithful. Yet even on the day of their fasting they were exploiting their workers. Their fasting would often end in quarreling and strife and in inflicting physical violence on each other. Old Testament law was a divine revelation of good, teaching Israel how to love God and their neighbors.[8] The following passage from Isaiah illustrates the point.

"Is this the kind of fast I have chosen, only a day for a man to humble himself? Is it only for bowing one's head like a reed and for lying on sackcloth and ashes? Is that what you call a fast, a day acceptable to the Lord? Is not this the kind of fasting I have chosen:

---

[5]Ibid.
[6]Ibid., 368.
[7]Ibid., 369.
[8]Ibid.

to loose the chains of injustice and untie the cords of the yoke, to set the oppressed free and break every yoke? Is it not to share your food with the hungry and to provide the poor wanderer with shelter—when you see the naked, to clothe him, and not to turn away from your own flesh and blood? Then your light will break forth like the dawn, and your healing will quickly appear; then your righteousness will go before you, and the glory of the Lord will be your rear guard. Then you will call, and the Lord will answer; you will cry for help, and he will say: Here am I. If you do away with the yoke of oppression, with the pointing finger and malicious talk, and if you spend yourselves in behalf of the hungry and satisfy the needs of the oppressed, then your light will rise in the darkness, and your night will become like the noonday" (Isa. 58:5-10).

Social ministers may find comfort in that what God calls justice is the domain of social ministry. Social ministry's contribution to the body of Christ and to the nation has an impact upon our relationship to God. God calls humanity to do justice. God chooses to use social ministers as His spokespersons. Just societies and just individuals fulfill God's will by meeting the needs of the powerless and defending the oppressed. When individuals and societies fail to do this, God's justice calls upon Him to implement His judgment on the evildoers.[9]

Mercy

Mercy is a key concept in the Old Testament. Being merciful is a part of the commitment one makes to God in the fulfillment of His law of righteousness. In Hebrew three words are translated *mercy*: *hesed*, which means kindness; *raham*, which refers to bowels; and *hanan*, which is also translated as *gracious*. In the *Pictoral Bible Dictionary* mercy is defined as: (1) Forbearance from inflicting punishment upon an adversary or a lawbreaker. (2) Compassion which causes one to help the weak, the sick, or the poor.[10] *Baker's Dictionary of Theology* states that mercy is a communicable attribute of God. It expresses God's goodness and love for the guilty and miserable. Pity, compassion, gentleness, and forbearance are also included. It is free and absolute.[11]

The first act of mercy recorded in the Bible immediately follows the fall: God clothes Adam and Eve with animal skins (Gen.

[9]Ibid.

[10]Merrill C. Tenney, ed., *Pictoral Bible Dictionary* (Nashville: Southwestern Company, 1966), 525.

[11]Everett F. Harrison, ed. *Baker's Dictionary of Theology* (Grand Rapids: Baker Book House, 1960), 348.

3:21). Some writers have suggested that this action represents the covering of our sins by the work of Christ, but that is not the only reason for God's action. After the fall, humans needed protection from a hostile environment. Derek Kidner said, "Social action could not have had an earlier or more exalted inauguration" than to have the Creator Himself provide for the clothing and protection of sinful human beings.[12]

Even before giving the law to Moses, God made His will known concerning social ministry. Job, who lived in a pre-Mosaic age, knew that the righteousness God requires includes providing food, shelter, and clothing to the needy (Job 24:1-21; 31:16-23). In fact, Job said that he did more than simple social service. "I was a father to the needy; I took up the case of the stranger. I broke the fangs of the wicked and snatched the victims from their teeth" (Job 29:16-17).[13]

When God gave the law to Moses, He was constructing a believing community in which social righteousness was a requirement, just as were personal righteousness and morality. Individual Israelites were forbidden to harvest all their produce, so the poor could glean from the fields for free (Ex. 23:10-11). Israelites were told to give to the poor until the poor person's need was gone (Deut. 15:8,10), especially if the poor was a kinsman or a neighbor (Lev. 25:25,35-38). Priests gave to the poor out of the tithes to God (Deut. 14:28-29).[14]

God's law required that the poor be given more than a handout. When a slave was freed from debt and servitude, he was not to leave empty-handed, but had to be given grain or livestock so that he could become economically self-sufficient (Deut. 15:12-15). The laws given to Moses were the basis for the thundering of the later prophets, who denounced Israel's insensitivity to the poor as breaking covenant with God. They taught that materialism and the ignoring of the poor's plight are sins as repugnant to God as idolatry and adultery (Amos 2:6-7). Mercy to the poor is an evidence of a true heart.[15]

Love

Aheb. The Hebrew word *aheb* is the word most commonly translated "love" in the Old Testament. This is a general word for

---

[12]Quoted by Timothy Keller, *Ministries of Mercy: The Call of the Jericho Road* (Grand Rapids: Zondervan Publishing House, 1989), 41.
[13]Ibid.
[14]Ibid.
[15]Ibid.

love or like, and it varies in intensity with its subject and its object. For example, *aheb* is used with reference to the relationship between a father and son (Gen. 22:2; 44:20) and a slave and master (Ex. 21:5). Most importantly for the social minister, it is the word used in the commandment regarding love for neighbor (Lev. 19:18) and for the stranger as well (Deut. 10:19). This is the word used when the Hebrew speaks of human love for God, and it is often used to indicate God's love for people. Richards stated that when this word is used of God's love, the character of God infuses it with intensity and stability (Jer. 31:3).[16] In like manner, when God calls social ministers to do His work, they become the incarnation of God's *aheb* in the church and the community.

Almost every human being has been endowed with this type of love. However, when humans love in this way they can easily reach a limit; their love takes on a conditional quality. On the other hand, when God engenders this type of love, He infuses it with a depth and breadth beyond the reach of a human being. Social ministries draw on love of neighbors and strangers as a source of motivation. The minister who engages in service activities does so out of an inner-directed drive that says, "You are important and I care about you. I enjoy helping you."

When the person being helped is ungrateful, unlovely, obnoxious, pushy, demanding, and rude, the social minister may easily reach the limit of his or her ability to love. It is at this point that the incarnation of God's love becomes an essential quality for social ministers. Here their motives in serving go beyond the human dimension and take on acts of mercy because this is what God wants His ministers to do. Incarnational ministers are not limited by human caring. When the depths of human caring are reached, Christian social ministers are able to tap the limitless depths of God's love and continue to serve.

Hesed. The *New International Version* of the Bible also translates *hesed* "love" or "kindness." The *New American Standard Bible* renders this term "lovingkindness." Among people, *hesed* describes a bond of loyalty, such as is established between relatives, friends, or allies. An act of *hesed* is carried out by free choice in harmony with the relationship; thus *hesed* is an expression of love appropriate to a relationship. The term is theologically significant because it is often used to express divine attitudes and actions. It was God's deep love that moved him to establish covenants with humans in

---

[16]Richards, *Expository Dictionary*, 418.

the first place.[17] For social ministers, relationships are very important. Helping is accomplished through relationships. Acts of kindness initiated by social ministers indicate that the clients are important. This type of love also conveys to clients that social ministers can be trusted. The relationship will be consistent; that is, every time clients encounter social ministers they will always receive the same level of acceptance. When social ministers become the incarnation of God's love (*hesed*), they demonstrate qualities that indicate that clients are more than names on a chart. Clients are not simply obligations, but persons who are loved, first by God, and also by social ministers. Incarnational ministers will not be passive in the relationship. In the likeness of the heavenly Father, they will take the initiative to be helpful to their clients.

Raham. Another word translated "love" is *raham*, which is also translated "compassion."[18] The root refers to a deep love rooted in some "natural" bond. In its denominative verb form it connotes the mercy that persons feel for one another because they are human beings (Jer. 50:42). Mercy is elicited for small babies (Isa. 13:18) or other helpless people. *Raham* is frequently used with reference to God. It can refer to the compassion God has for his children (Ps. 103:13) when he looks down on them and has pity on them (Mic. 7:19). Also, *raham* indicates that God has compassion and is gracious and merciful to whomever He chooses (Ex. 33:19).[19]

For the social minister, the human condition creates powerful emotional reactions. First, this type of love or compassion is the source of empathy. *Empathy,* an essential quality possessed by effective social ministers, refers to feeling with the hurting person. It refers to understanding what the hurting person is feeling. It refers to caring that the hurting person is hurting. Second, the incarnational minister chooses to have compassion on and minister to any person whom God loves. This includes any person God has created and for whom God's only begotten Son died.

Only in Jeremiah 2:2 do we find love (*hesed*) used of humanity's response to God. We sense that love's expression is primarily an obedience that demonstrates one's clinging to the Lord. Moses' admonition to the people to "love the Lord your God with all your heart and with all your soul and with all your strength" (Deut. 6:5) uses the Hebrew word *aheb*. This commandment is fulfilled by

---

[17]Ibid., 419.
[18]Ibid.
[19]R. Laird Harris, Gleason L. Archer, and Bruce K. Waltke, eds. *Theological Wordbook of the Old Testament*, vol. 2 (Chicago: Moody Press, 1980), 841-842.

being obedient (Deut. 6:6). The relationship between human love for God and obedience to His will is seen in many places in the Old Testament (Deut. 30:16-20; Josh. 22:5; see also Ps. 119:113, 119, 127, 159, 163, 165, 167).[20] What God wills comes out of His character. He is always righteous, just, merciful, and loving. Incarnational social ministers will always practice righteousness, justice, mercy, and love as reflections of God's nature and in obedience to His call.

New Testament Foundations

Understanding the historical background and Old Testament foundational concepts that undergird Christian social ministry is very important. However, for most evangelical Christians, establishing a New Testament foundation is more important.

The Love Cornerstone

Love is the central motif, perfectly manifested in Jesus Christ, actualized by the Holy Spirit in the life of the Christian, and oriented toward people in the concrete situation. To love means to will the welfare of others. Any action, attitude, ideology, or system that hurts people and hinders them from reaching a state of well-being stands under the judgment of love.[21]

For the Christian, love that is translated into action regarding human needs is not something you catch, like a cold, or do if you feel like it; it is commanded as a response to God's love. Delamarter reminded us that the entire helping stance of the Christian is grounded in the nature and activity of God.[22] This concept is borne out in the statement "We love [God] because he first loved us . . . And he has given us this command: Whoever loves God must also love his brother" (1 John 4:19,21). We are also told that "love comes from God. Everyone who loves has been born of God and knows God" (1 John 4:7-8). Jesus was very specific about our relationship with Him: "If you love me, you will obey what I command" (John 14:15).

God's mercy, justice, and righteousness all come together in the concept of love revealed in the Old and New Testaments. However, when Jesus was born, lived, ministered, died, rose from the grave, and ascended to heaven, He revealed a dimension of love

---

[20]Richards, *Expository Dictionary*, 420.
[21]Henlee H. Barnette, *Crucial Problems in Christian Perspective* (Philadelphia: Westminster Press, 1970), 21.
[22]Walter Delamarter, *The Diakonic Task* (Atlanta: Home Mission Board, 1970), 38.

that surpasses anything the Old Testament writers could have known. While the Old Testament speaks more of justice and righteousness administered with mercy, the New Testament speaks more of the love of God which includes all of these qualities. All that God does grows out of His limitless love (John 3:16; 17:23-24; Rom. 5:5, 8; Eph. 1:4; 2:4; 3:18-19; 1 John 2:5; 3:1; 4:8-9, 16-17).

Jesus is the embodiment of God's love. His teachings provide a perspective that continues to inform those who would be His followers. Most of the work and teachings of Jesus, documented in the New Testament, consist of what we call social ministry. They deal directly with the physical, relational, and emotional needs of people. Of course, they also deal with the spiritual as well. Jesus indicated that He was expressing God's love (John 3:16). The writings of Paul, Peter, James, Jude, and John make much of the human being's social responsibilities. These ministries are considered synonymous with worshiping God (Gal. 6:1-2; Heb. 13:15-16; Jas. 1:27; 1 Pet. 2:12; 1 John 3:14-17; Jude 23; Rev. 2:19).

John recorded the prayer of Jesus for His followers, giving a specific clue about what will be expected of us (John 17). John 17:18 states, "As thou hast sent me into the world, even so have I sent them into the world" (KJV). We might assume from this statement that He was speaking of being sent; however, this would be inconsistent with His instructions in other passages. For example, in John 14:12 He said, "Verily, verily, I say unto you, He that believeth on me, the works that I do shall he do also; and greater works than these shall he do; because I go unto my Father"(KJV).

Another example is contained in the Great Commission. The Christian is not only to "teach all nations, baptizing them" (Matt. 28:19, KJV), but the subject is "all things whatsoever I have commanded you" (Matt. 28:20, KJV). Mark's version of the Great Commission includes a more specific ministry directive: "Go into all the world and preach the good news to all creation. . . . In my name they will drive out demons. . . . They will place their hands on sick people, and they will get well" (Mark 16:15, 17-18, NIV).

Obviously, the good news of the forgiveness of sin and eternal life is primary in the message of the Christian. However, the good news is incomplete if there is only hope for the future and no concern for the physical, emotional, and relational problems of contemporary life. Jesus is the role model for the social minister in both action and attitude. He gave much of His energy to meeting the temporal needs of the persons He encountered as he taught them about eternal matters. He modeled an attitude of unselfish service (Mark 10:45). He felt that the most powerful witness to His messiahship was His service. When John the Baptist sought evidence of Jesus' authenticity, He told John's disciples to "Go back and report to John what you hear and see: The blind receive sight, the lame walk, those who have leprosy are cured, the deaf hear, the dead are raised, and the good news is preached to the poor" (Matt. 11:4-5, NIV).

There was a concreteness in Christ's own ministry. This is evidenced by the fact that we have specific details about his work with many needy persons. His ministry was more than a mere concern for social action. This is especially true if the social action fails to get down to the everyday life. Christian social action does have its roots in the teachings of Christ and has a viable role to play in the schema of social ministry. However, when the impact of action strategies upon individual persons is ignored and emphasis is placed solely upon changing social systems, it violates Christ's model.

Thus, the Christian social minister is not as much concerned about changing social systems at the *macrosystems* level as at the *microsystems* level. In other words, while Christ taught principles which were revolutionary when advocated in societal institutions (macrosystems), His primary method was to work with individuals and small groups (microsystems). Changed individuals make up changed groups, and changed groups become a force for changing society.

For example, when Jesus was visiting a synagogue He was handed a scroll of the prophet Isaiah. He read, "The Spirit of the Lord is on me; because He has anointed me to preach good news to the poor. He has sent me to proclaim freedom for the prisoners and recovery of sight for the blind, to release the oppressed, to proclaim the year of the Lord's favor!" (Luke 4:18-19, NIV). When He finished reading He told the audience, "Today this scripture is fulfilled in your hearing" (Luke 4:21). There are both macrosystemic and microsystemic implications in the prophecy, and the expected results are changes in both.

When we follow the life of Jesus and observe His works in the gospels, we see Him preaching to the poor in groups, healing individuals, deploring unfair practices, identifying with the outcast and powerless, and, on occasion, confronting the religious power structure in their domain. His primary mission always contained a personal element in the context of His overarching purpose, which had definite macrocosmic implications. While the world was the object of His coming, "For God so loved the world," the good news always focuses upon the individual, "that whosoever" (John 3:16, KJV). Thus the ministry of Christ and that of contemporary social ministers is macrocosmic in scope, but the method is microsystemic in focus. As Christ focused His concern for all humankind, including the totality of every person's being, it is the responsibility of the Christian social minister to concentrate on the total needs of individuals in the same Spirit.

God's love and the Christian's incarnation of that love is the primary cornerstone for all ministry. This is especially true of social ministry. If we had no concept other than the love of God as a motive for social ministry, it would be sufficient. The term *incarnation* comes from the Latin word meaning "becoming flesh" or "becoming human."[23] Incarnation carries with it the idea of embodying the concept. Thus the social minister becomes the embodiment of the love of God in relationships with other human beings, in grateful response to God's love. The apostle Paul specifically spoke of the incarnational Christian in Colossians 1:27, in which he referred to "Christ in you, the hope of glory" (KJV).

The Language of Love in the New Testament

To understand love as a New Testament cornerstone for Christian social ministry, it would be useful to discuss the various meanings of the word *love*. The English language uses only one word for love, and that word has many meanings. Greek, the original language of the New Testament, used different words for love which allowed a writer or speaker to be more precise. These words were *phileo, agapao,* and *eros. Eros* referred to love based on the value of the object, but it is not found in the Greek Testament. The Greek verb *agapao* was a little-used word until Christians began to infuse it with great meaning. Vine stated that it was the characteristic word of Christianity. A study of the word in classical or historical literature, other than the Bible, will shed little light on its meaning. The New Testament provides the greatest understanding of the meaning of *agapao*.

The noun *agape* and the verb *agapao* are used in the New Testament to describe the attitude of God toward His Son (John 17:26), humanity (John 3:16; Rom. 5:8), and any who believe in Jesus Christ

---

[23]Tenney, *Pictorial Bible Dictionary,* 373.

(John 14:21). The word was also used to convey God's will concerning Christians in their relationships with each other and with all persons (John 13:34; 1 Cor. 16:14; 1 Thess. 3:12; 2 Pet. 1:7). This is the word most applicable to social ministry because agape love can only be known from the actions it prompts. God's own action is seen in the gift of His Son (1 John 4:9-10). This type of love is then shown in the fruit of the Spirit (Gal. 5:22). For the Christian social minister, this love is exercised toward all persons, especially those of the household of faith (Rom. 13:8-10; 15:2; 1 Cor. 13; Gal. 6:10; Col. 3:12-14).[24] It is this type of love that is commanded in the "great love commandment" (Matt. 22:37-40; Mark 12:28-34; Luke 10:25-28).

Phileo and philia were the most common words for love in Greek in the New Testament times. They most nearly represent what could be called tender affection. Although phileo may be encouraged, it is not the kind of love that is commanded. Phileo is sometimes used along with agapao to describe the love of the Father for the Son (John 3:35; 5:20) and for the believer (John 14:21; 16:27). Vine stated that there is a distinction between the two verbs and that they always retain their distinctives. They are never used indiscriminately in the same passage. When the two appear in the same passage with reference to the same objects, each retains its distinctive and essential character.[25] The impact of the love concept contained in phileo is that it conveys the thought of cherishing the object of love above all else. It manifests an affection characterized by constancy.[26] This speaks of the social minister's quality of commitment to God and empathy for the client.

The noun agape speaks of God's character, for "God is love" (1 John 4:8,16). It also speaks of the Christian's identification with God's character (1 John 4:17). As long as the social minister is in the world, he or she is the incarnation of God's character, which is best described as unselfish, self-giving, enduring, and aggressive love.[27]

A compound noun using this root is philanthropia which literally means love for humans. This word refers to the qualities of kindness and compassion. While these qualities are not commanded, they are encouraged.[28] A social minister who does not feel

---

[24]W. E. Vine, An Expository Dictionary of New Testament Words, vol. 3 (Old Tappan, N.J.: Fleming H. Revell Company, 1966), 20-21.

[25]Ibid., 21.

[26]Ibid., 22.

[27]Ibid.

[28]Ibid.

compassion and kindness toward persons in need will not be very effective.

The Love Commandment

If we look for a scriptural stack-pole around which to construct a biblical basis for social ministry, no greater one can be found than the Great Commandment, quoted by Jesus in Matthew and Mark and discussed in Luke. The Matthew account states that Jesus was approached by a group attempting to trip him up. They asked which was the first and greatest commandment in the Scriptures.

Jesus, quoting Deuteronomy 6:5 and Leviticus 19:18, answered: "Thou shalt love the Lord thy God with all thy heart, and with all thy soul, and with all thy mind. This is the first and great commandment. And the second is like unto it, Thou shalt love thy neighbour as thyself. On these two commandments hang all the law and the prophets" (Matt. 22:37-40, KJV).

The Mark version includes additional insights: "The first of all the commandments is, Hear, O Israel; the Lord our God is one Lord: And thou shalt love the Lord thy God with all thy heart, and with all thy soul, and with all thy mind, and with all thy strength: this is the first commandment. And the second is like unto it, namely this, Thou shalt love thy neighbour as thyself. There is none other commandment greater than these" (Mark 12:29-31, KJV).

In the Luke account, Jesus asked the lawyer to quote the law. The lawyer rendered the following: "Thou shalt love the Lord thy God with all thy heart, and with all thy soul, and with all thy strength, and with all thy mind; and thy neighbour as thyself" (Luke 10:25-27, KJV).

Love of God. The biblical basis for social ministry begins with an *agape* relationship with the Lord our God. It is a commandment rooted in the fact that God loves in the same manner. God's actions thereby call for an in-kind response from Christians. Our response is to be one of total commitment and submission to the will of God. We please God most when we choose to carry out His purpose and plan in our lives (1 Sam. 15:22; Matt. 28:20; Luke 11:28).

Self-seeking behavior is the opposite of the *agape* form of love. When people's prayers are purely selfish or manipulative, their praying is more akin to *eros* than to Christian love. The *eros* concept of love finds expression in the attitude "What can I get for me?" or "I'm looking out for number 1." These expressions are very subtle when they come in religious or "spiritual" garb. Used in the religious context these phrases are, "It did so much *for me* that nothing had ever done before" or, "I want to go to a church where I will be fed spiritually."

Agape, on the other hand, calls for serious introspection to "see if there be any wicked way in me" (Ps. 139:24, KJV). The attitude that brings ultimate joy to the Christian is expressed in, "How precious also are thy thoughts unto me, O God! How great is the sum of them!" (Ps. 139:17, KJV). However, if these thoughts and expressions are not translated into action—doing the will of God— one must suspect that the motive is not *agape* but *eros*. Instead of seeking a church where one can be "fed" or where one gets so much out of the ministries offered, Christian love calls for one to seek a church where one can serve. The *agape* attitude is not what "it" does for me, but what I can do for others.

Jesus provided us with an excellent example of the appropriate attitude: "My food is to do the will of Him who sent me and to finish his work" (John 4:34). President John F. Kennedy expressed this attitude in his inaugural address: "Ask not what your country can do for you; ask what you can do for your country." The love commitment is not simply an idealistic, immature, andor emotional proclamation. It involves an act of rational will. It comes from the very center of the Christian's being, *the heart*. In Jewish thought the heart was the seat of thinking and feeling; therefore, the love commandment calls for an emotional and rational commitment from the believer.[29]

Closely aligned with the heart is loving God with "all your *soul*"; this involves all that a person is: natural body, personality, and emotions. A person's perceptions, feelings, desires, and will are facets of the soul.

Paralleling the heart and soul is the *mind*. The mind is used in reference to understanding and intelligence. Thus our understanding and mental capacities are to be at God's disposal.[30]

Mark and Luke add *might* andor *strength* to round out the totality of human existence. These are to be committed to God in love. All that a human is, feels, thinks, wills, and does is required in love-service to God.

---

[29]Frank Stagg, "Matthew," *Broadman Bible Commentary*, Vol. 8 (Nashville: Broadman Press, 1969), 209.

[30]Henry E. Turlington, "Mark," *Broadman Bible Commentary*, Vol. 8 (Nashville: Broadman Press, 1969), 366.

Second and of equal importance. Immediately following the quotation from Deuteronomy 6:5, and Leviticus 19:18, "You shall love your neighbor as yourself," Jesus stated that the second commandment is just like the first (Matt. 22:39; Mark 12:31). Very likely this means that it is *equal* in importance, as indicated in the statement, "On these two commandments depend the whole Law and the Prophets" (Matt. 22:40, NASB). The same degree of love one professes toward God is to be directed toward the neighbor.

From the Matthew version we can conclude that these two commandments do not just contain the law; they constitute it. They provide the decisive word about its meaning and thus enable us to determine its correct interpretation. This would be consistent with the meaning of the passage in Leviticus.[31] T. B. Maston reminded us that this passage is a quotation from the Old Testament. In Leviticus, immediately following the command to be holy, instructions concerning how to relate to family members and others, and how to perform rituals, there is a statement summing up all that has gone before: "Thou shalt love thy neighbour as thyself" (Lev. 19:1-18, KJV).[32] Christ's interpretation is in keeping with the spirit of the original Old Testament message.

Commenting on the Mark passage, Furnish stated that in effect Jesus was telling the scribe that no one commandment can be marked as "first," but that these together (love of God and love of neighbor) constitute the essence of the law. The second commandment is not necessarily second in importance for understanding the law. The union of the singular "no other commandment" and the plural "than these" maintains the distinction between the two precepts but puts them into a special category. They are not ranked but listed.[33] Neither commandment is complete without the other. No one can love God supremely and not love those whom God loves. On the other hand, one cannot love a neighbor with a love that partakes of the divine quality without loving God supremely.[34]

Love of neighbor. There are three Greek words for neighbor: *geiton* which refers to one living in the same land; *perioikos* meaning one dwelling around; and *plesion* which means the one near. The word used in the Great Commandment is *plesion*, which indicates that the neighbor the Christian is to love is anyone who is nearby.

---

[31]Victor Furnish, *The Love Commandment in the New Testament* (Nashville: Abingdon Press, 1974), 34.

[32]T. B. Maston, *Biblical Ethics* (Waco: Word Books, 1967), 26.

[33]Furnish, *The Love Commandment*, 26-27.

[34]Maston, *Biblical Ethics*, 149-150.

This teaching was, no doubt, radical to the Pharisees. For them a neighbor would be another Pharisee. They called themselves *Haberion*, which was sometimes translated "neighbors." To think of anyone who happened to be near as the recipient of an *agape* love response would be very foreign to this elitist sect.[35]

Of the three accounts we have in the Gospels, the Book of Luke provides us with the most apt discussion of the concept of neighbor love. After the lawyer had quoted the laws, he still wanted to justify himself, "so he asked Jesus, and who is my neighbor?" (Luke 10:29). The question implies that he wanted a definition. In reply Jesus told him the story of the Good Samaritan (Luke 10:30-35). He concluded His answer by asking, " 'Which of these three do you think was a neighbor to the man who fell into the hands of robbers?' The expert in the law replied, 'The one who had mercy on him' " (Luke 10:36-37).

In telling this parable, Jesus, as He had done in Matthew and Mark, went beyond what the question asked. He did something imminently more practical in three ways. First, He avoided an intellectual or formal answer to the question, "Who is my neighbor?" in that He did not define "neighbor" as a class of neighbors distinguished from a class of nonneighbors (as the Pharisees would do). Rather, He described what a neighbor does.[36] Second, instead of giving a definition enabling one to recognize neighbors as opposed to nonneighbors, He set an example demanding that one concentrate on being a neighbor to others—whomever they may be. Third, in His parable the position and status of the Christian becomes less and less important. Being a person to whom the law of love lays claim becomes more important.

Finally, the lawyer was forced to discern the meaning of love of neighbor in very concrete terms and to feel the ultimate effect of the claims of the "Great Commandment" on his own behavior as a person under God's law. The lawyer was given a dramatic illustration of what obedience to the law actually means—in reality, what it *must* mean for *him*.[37]

Perhaps Perrin summed up the impact of the Good Samaritan story in stating that the lawyer's question was clearly answered. The command to love the neighbor breaks down all barriers that divide humanity. Neighbor love means helping the person who needs help, regardless of who he or she is in relation to

---

[35]Frank Stagg, "Matthew," 209.
[36]Furnish, *The Love Commandment*, 60.
[37]Ibid., 42.

oneself.[38] It is also noteworthy that Jesus' final statement to the lawyer (and also to us) is an imperative command: "Go and do likewise" (Luke 10:37).

Love of self. Although the emphasis of the Great Commandment is on loving God and neighbor, there is an assumption implied in the statement, "Love your neighbor as yourself." Frank Stagg pointed out that there is a self-love that is depravity, but there is also a godly love that necessarily includes oneself. When we realize that we are God's as well as our neighbor's, we find that we must also be true to ourselves. Either we love God, neighbor, *and* self, or we do not love God or neighbor.[39]

The Golden Rule is also built upon the idea of loving oneself. Luke 6:31 is the famous verse: "Do to others as you would have them to do to you" (NIV). It is a positive treatment of an old maxim known among Jews and Gentiles alike. It was usually stated negatively: "What you do not want others to do unto you, do not do unto them." By turning this negative statement into a positive one, Christ determined in a more absolute form how we should act toward our neighbors.[40]

Because of its positive nature it is action oriented rather than reactionary ("Do to others"). It is qualitative ("as you would have them do to you"), meaning in the same manner, the same form, the same amount, with the same respect, the same attitude, and the same consistency as you would want them to treat you if you needed help. It is the essence of acceptance of the other person, in love that does not judge, blame, grow impatient, or manipulate (see 1 Cor. 13). Our relationship to others has a direct relationship to our own self-concepts. What we want for ourselves, qualitatively, we should be prepared to do for others. This is not just a human-relations maxim: it implies a service delivered to our neighbors, thereby becoming a chief cornerstone for the practice of social ministry.

Love of enemies. Just how far does this love take us in ministering to persons? What does Jesus require of the Christian as a helper and as a neighbor? Perhaps we can find the limits of our service in Luke 6:27-30; 35-36: "But I tell you who hear me: Love your enemies, do good to those who hate you, bless those who curse you,

---

[38]Norman Perrin, *Rediscovering the Teaching of Jesus* (New York: Harper and Row, 1967), 124.

[39]Stagg, "Matthew," 209-210.

[40]Norva Geldenhys, *Commentary on the Gospel of Luke* (Grand Rapids: Wm. B. Eerdmans Publishing Co., 1977), 212.

pray for those who mistreat you. If someone strikes you on one cheek, turn him the other also. If someone takes your cloak, do not stop him from taking your tunic. Give to everyone who asks you, and if anyone takes what belongs to you, do not demand it back.... But love your enemies, do good to them, and lend to them without expecting to get anything back. Then your reward will be great, and you will be sons of the Most High, because he is kind to the ungrateful and wicked. Be merciful, just as your father is merciful."

It is probably this commandment to *love your enemies* that sets Jesus' ethic of love apart from all other "love ethics." This passage suggests that love for God means more than being obedient to his commands, as a child obeys a parent. It means to be *like* God in loving even those who have turned against Him. Notice that Jesus not only had love for His enemies, but also commanded it of His followers. The net result of one's *agape* love, even for enemies, is that more is done than recognizing that another person exists. The commandment precludes our ignoring another person and insists upon affirming the person constructively as well as compassionately.[41]

Another important aspect of this commandment, which is consistent with the concept of *agape*, is that what is done for the neighbor is not conditioned upon a reciprocal act by the neighbor (Luke 6:35). In this lack of expectation we are following the example of our Lord, who is merciful even to those who hate Him (Luke 6:36; Matt. 5:45).

Paul and the Love Commandment

Romans 12:15. Paul discussed the love relationship of fellow believers with the same concreteness that Jesus emphasized in his teachings: "Be devoted to one another in brotherly love. Honor one another above yourselves.... Share with God's people who are in need. Practice hospitality. Bless those who persecute you; bless and do not curse.... Do not be proud, but be willing to associate with people of low position. Do not repay anyone evil for evil.... On the contrary: If your enemy is hungry, feed him; if he is thirsty, give him something to drink" (Rom. 12:10-20).

Paul used a compound form of *phileo* in verse 10, suggesting the qualities of devotion and honor in our relationships with brothers and sisters in Christ. Throughout his writings, Paul stressed the fact that the witness of God's people is not composed just of verbal expression, but also includes the actions of believers as a caring fel-

[41]Furnish, *The Love Commandment*, 66.

lowship (see Rom. 14—15). This witness is threefold in that it includes a verbal witness, a testimony of a caring fellowship, and a demonstration of God's love working through those who are "in Christ" to minister to the needs of those who are not a part of the "in-group."

This passage gives us a clear picture of Paul's concept of loving neighbors, including one's enemies. He thus explicitly carried forward the teachings and example of Christ. This relationship with the enemy is to include rejoicing, mourning, living in harmony, and accepting the person as an equal. Some commentators feel that there was a mistake in copying Romans 12. They speculate that verse 14 should have come after verse 16 and that verses 15-16 belong with Paul's instructions regarding our relationships with fellow Christians. However, from what we have seen in the Gospels regarding *agape* love, the Golden Rule, and loving one's enemies, verses 15-16 seem to be confirmations of God's will regarding our relationships with all our neighbors, especially our enemies. In carrying out these instructions, we will "overcome evil with good" (Rom. 12:21, KVJ).[42]

Paul taught that love is both the context and content of faith, God's love makes faith possible, and human love gives it visibility and effect in the world.[43] This is borne out in Romans 13, where he discussed the personal conduct of the Christian in the world: "Give everyone what you owe him: if you owe taxes, pay taxes; if revenue, then revenue; if respect, then respect; if honor, then honor. Let no debt remain outstanding, except the continuing debt to love one another, for he who loves his fellowman has fulfilled the law. . . . Love does no harm to its neighbor. Therefore love is the fulfillment of the law. And do this, understanding the present time. The hour has come for you to wake up from your slumber, because our salvation is nearer now than when we first believed. . . . Rather, clothe yourselves with the Lord Jesus Christ, and do not think about how to gratify the desires of the sinful nature" (Rom. 13:7-8,10-11,14).

Here the apostle reiterated the basic commandments in a manner similar to Christ's in the Gospels and interjected an eschatological element in verse 11. He concluded by explaining the daily moral walk of the Christian in light of the eschatological moment. Paul apparently felt that time was short and that there was an urgency regarding our witness to a lost and dying world. That

---

[42]Dale Moody, "Romans," *Broadman Bible Commentary*, Vol. 10 (Nashville: Broadman Press, 1970), 250.

[43]Furnish, *The Love Commandment*, 94.

urgency continues to exist from several perspectives. For the social minister, one perspective is that time is precious and people's needs are immediate. Another is that the Christian's primary concern should be for making the most of every opportunity to help persons in need as opposed to wasting precious time and energy on acquiring temporal benefits for oneself. Storing up treasures in heaven is much more important.

Romans 14:1—15:3 relates to helping fellow believers who are not mature in the faith. In love, judgment is prohibited. Christians are to bear with or tolerate the failings of the weak and not be selfish in performing desired activities. These may not be understood by the weaker brothers; therefore, they become stumbling blocks to them. "Each of us should please his neighbor for his good, to build him up. For even Christ did not please himself but, as it is written: 'The insults of those who insult you have fallen on me'" (Rom. 15:2-3). By "pleasing others" he did not mean that we are to be so sensitive to the desires of persons that we conform to their every whim. That would constitute an unhealthy behavior known as codependency. But we should respect persons in such a way that we affirm them as having worth.

Galatians 5—6. In the Galatians letter Paul specifically dealt with the contrast of law and grace. His specific emphasis was that justification is by grace through faith and that we are free in Christ. He warned, however, that we are not to use our freedom to indulge our sinful natures (Gal. 5:13). This would be the opposite of love because those sinful things violate the *agape* principle with regard to God or neighbor (or both). We should "rather serve one another in love. The entire law is summed up in a single command: 'Love your neighbor as yourself'" (Gal. 5:13b-14). Notice that Paul did not include the Deuteronomy passage here, but he apparently felt that our faith in Christ and adherence to the love commandment regarding our neighbors would indeed fulfill the command to love God.

Galatians 6 gives us potent instructions about how the Christians should carry out the love commandment. Paul began by admonishing spiritual persons to gently restore the one trapped in sin, being careful not to allow themselves to be tempted (Gal. 6:1). Then Paul broadened the concern to carrying each other's burdens and in this way fulfilling the law of Christ (Gal. 6:2). Almost as an afterthought, it seems, Paul gave instructions about personal responsibility: "Each one should test his own actions . . . for each one should carry his own load" (vv. 4-5). In the light of love, both for God and others, we must guard our actions and carry our own weight. However, if there are weaker brothers or sisters in the fellowship, they are not to be judged (Rom. 14:1) but to be lifted up in prayer and allowed to maintain their own integrity by evaluating their own actions and doing what they can for themselves and others. Persons are not to remain dependent upon others.

Another significant passage to the social minister—indeed, to any Christian—is Galatians 6:10: "Therefore, as we have opportunity, let us do good to all people, especially to those who belong to the family of believers." This passage sums up the Christian's responsibility for persons inside and outside the community of faith. The tenor of the passage is one in which the Christian takes the initiative. Note also that this passage follows one about sowing and reaping: sowing to the flesh and reaping corruption; sowing to the spirit and reaping life eternal. Now, in verse 10, the Christian is to do a unique kind of planting.[44] Planting the seed of helping leads to a harvest of goodwill. It is the most powerful witness practiced by Christians at any time. It breaks down the barriers that prevent one coming to know and accept Christ as Savior.

The phrase "as we have opportunity" does not mean that we should do good if we happen to be near or if doing so is convenient. It implies that social ministers are to take the initiative and be alert for opportunities to do good. The word *do* is from *ergazomai*, which emphasizes the process of an action. It means "to labor, to be active, to perform," with the idea of continued exertion.[45] There is nothing passive about this commandment. What is at stake is not a single occasion but the whole lifespan of the Christian helper.[46] The overarching phrase "to all people" is obviously in keeping with the "law of Christ" in 6:2, and to the example Christ set as He ate with the Pharisees (Luke 7:36-50) and publicans (Luke 19:1-10) as well as friends (Luke 10:38-42). And it is in keeping with His teachings regarding love of neighbors.[47]

The act of doing good is to be directed to everyone; there was, however, some gradation in the admonition. The household of

---

[44]John W. MacGorman, "Galatians," *Broadman Bible Commentary*, Vol. 11 (Nashville: Broadman Press, 1971), 123.

[45]Kenneth S. Wuest, *Galatians in the Greek New Testament* (Grand Rapids: Wm. B. Eerdmans Publishing Co., 1944), 174.

[46]Herman N. Ridderbos, *The Epistle of Paul to the Churches of Galatia* (Grand Rapids: Wm. B. Eerdmans Publishing Co., 1953), 220.

[47]MacGorman, "Galatians," 123.

faith was to be given first place. But exclusivism was to be avoided because it conflicts with the law of Christ.[48]

Paul confirmed doing good as a means of fulfilling God's law of love through the parallelism of 1 Corinthians 14:1 (Pursue [the way of] love!) and 1 Thessalonians 5:15 (Pursue [the way of] good!). In Romans 13:10 he defined love as doing no evil to one's neighbor. The form of the word translated *evil* in Romans 13:10 is an exact antonym to the word *good* in Galatians 6:9 and the verb *does* has the same root as the word *do* in Galatians 6:10.[49]

This same theme is carried forth in 1 Thessalonians 3:12 in Paul's prayer that the Lord will enable the members of the fellowship to abound in love for one another and *to all persons*. In 1 Thessalonians 5:15 he admonished them to do good to one another *and to all*.[50]

Ministry and Judgment

So far in this chapter we have discussed how God admonishes Christians to engage in *agape* love relationships and service with persons inside and outside the community of faith. He both commands and models the concept.

Most evangelical Christians would not argue the point. However, social ministry is generally looked upon as a secondary type of ministry in our churches. What we have seen in this chapter would indicate that in God's scheme of things, social ministry is to be given a much higher priority in the Christian's life. Ministries of love and mercy are not secondary or optional. In fact, the New Testament stresses the fact that God sees this type of ministry as a test of genuine Christianity. Almost every book in the New Testament contains a testimony to this fact. Writers such as James, John, and Matthew were more pointed than others. For example, 1 John 3:17-18 states that if a Christian has the ability to help and sees another in need, but does not help, there is a reason to question whether God's love is in that person. If God's love is really there, it will be expressed in deeds as well as words. In a more pointed way, James questioned whether a profession of faith that is not accompanied by ministries of love is genuine.

"Speak and act as those who are going to be judged by the law that gives freedom, because judgment without mercy will be shown to anyone who has not been merciful. Mercy triumphs over

---

[48]Ridderbos, *The Epistle of Paul*, 220.
[49]Furnish, *The Love Commandment*, 101.
[50]Ibid., 102.

68

judgment! What good is it, my brothers, if a man claims to have faith but has no deeds? Can such faith save him? Suppose a brother or sister is without clothes and daily food. If one of you says to him, 'Go, I wish you well; keep warm and well fed,' but does nothing about his physical needs, what good is it? In the same way, faith by itself, if it is not accompanied by action, is dead" (Jas. 2:12-17).

The James passage is consistent with Proverbs 14:31 and 19:17. There we are told that to ignore the needs of the poor is to sin against the Lord Himself. It is obvious that the poor and otherwise needy serve as a test for the authentic Christian. Our response to the needy demonstrates the genuineness of our relationship with God.[51]

James, John, and Isaiah (Isa. 1:10-17), point out that a sensitive social conscience and a life poured out in deeds of *agape* love to the needy is the inevitable outcome and sign of true faith. By such behavior God judges true love versus lip service.[52] In Matthew 25 Jesus specifically delineated the acts of mercy that God will use in the judging of all persons: "Then the King will say to those on his right, 'Come, you who are blessed by my Father; take your inheritance, the kingdom prepared for you since the creation of the world. For I was hungry and you gave me something to eat, I was thirsty and you gave me something to drink, I was a stranger and you invited me in, I needed clothes and you clothed me, I was sick and you looked after me, I was in prison and you came to visit me.' Then the righteous will answer him, 'Lord, when did we see you hungry and feed you, or thirsty and give you something to drink? When did we see you a stranger and invite you in, or needing clothes and clothe you? When did we see you sick or in prison and go to visit you?' The King will reply, 'I tell you the truth, whatever you did for one of the least of these brothers of mine, you did for me'" (Matt. 25:34-40).

When Jesus said, "Whatever you did for one of the least of these brothers of mine, you did for me," he was expanding on the concept stated in Proverbs 19:17, "He who is kind to the poor lends to the Lord." The James, John, and Isaiah passages also stress that a sensitive social conscience and a life poured out in deeds motivated by *agape* love is the expected outcome of true faith. God observes these actions and separates lip service from true faith.[53]

---

[51] Timothy Keller, *Ministries of Mercy*, 38-39.
[52] Ibid. 39.
[53] Ibid.

Some writers title the judgment discussed in Matthew 25 "The Judgment of the Nations" or "The Judgment of Gentiles." They identify three other judgments: the judgment of Israel (Ezek. 20:33-38), the judgment of the church (2 Cor. 5:10-11), and the judgment of the wicked (Rev. 20:11-15).[54] It is important to note that in the judgment of the church there is no indication of separating the saved from the lost. The criteria for judgment are the works of the Christian that please Christ.

We have already established that acts of mercy, motivated by *agape* love, are the works of the believer that please the Lord. Along with following after other gods, Israel was guilty of forgetting God's righteousness, justice, and mercy in their dealings with each other, particularly the helpless and otherwise needy. These violations were consistently highlighted by the prophets when they called the nation back to God.

The judgment discussed in Revelation 20 appears to be about the separation of the saved from the lost. The lost are judged by what they have done. In Matthew 25 Jesus also discussed the criteria for judging the lost: "'Whatever you did not do for one of the least of these, you did not do for me.' Then they will go away to eternal punishment, but the righteous to eternal life" (Matt. 25:45-46).

Whether there are several judgments or one judgment with many facets, there remains a significant truth: all will be judged. In addition to belief in Christ, the primary criteria for the judgment of true believers are the actions involved in social ministry.

Summary and Conclusions

It is obvious that if relationships in the church do not reflect love, then the witness to those outside will be ineffective. However, if love is demonstrated in the church *and* to those outside with the same concrete actions, Christians' witness will be effective.

It is also significant that these actions are not to be "on demand" but part of the ongoing activity of the fellowship. In ministering to others, the Christian does not wait until compelled by an outside force; love, from inside, is the compelling force. The love of God works through the Christian social minister to perform the acts of Christ for all persons, even the enemies of the church and of Christ. The result will be "coals of fire" heaped upon the heads of

---

[54]C. I. Scofield, *Oxford NIV Scofield Study Bible* (New York: Oxford University Press, 1984), 1012-1013.

the enemies, not as a motive but as a by-product of "overcoming evil with good."

The eschatological message is that when all persons appear in the final judgment, we will give account of how we have exercised *agape* love in our relationships with all persons. Being compassionate and caring will not earn salvation. However, if we truly believe, social ministries will be natural outgrowths of our commitment to Christ.

Barriers will be broken down. A holistic ministry will be developed, including the spiritual, physical, emotional, mental, and relational. Justice, righteousness, and mercy are encompassed by *agape* love.

Exercises for Review and Examination

1. List and discuss how the Old Testament concepts of righteousness, justice, mercy, and love relate to the incarnational social minister.

2. Using both Old and New Testament foundational concepts, construct a rationale for social ministry programs in the church.

3. Write a comparison of the two major words for love in the Greek New Testament.

4. Discuss the use of the words *heart, soul, mind,* and *strength* in the Mark version of the Great Commandment.

5. Write a one-page statement about the significance of the Good Samaritan story as an answer to the question, "Who is my neighbor?"

6. Discuss what Jesus meant when He said, "Upon these two commandments hang all the law and the prophets."

7. Write a paragraph about what Jesus meant by His statement, "the second is just like it."

8. According to Jesus and Paul, what is the Christian's responsibility to an enemy? Write a paragraph explaining your answer.

9. Discuss the relationship of Galatians 6:10 to the redemptive purpose of the Christian's behavior.

Chapter Four

Theological Foundations for Christian Social Ministry

Goal: A study of this chapter should enable the social minister to understand how the basic doctrines of the Christian faith relate to the helping process.

Objectives: The minister . . .

1. explains who God is and what God is not.
2. describes the qualities of God and how they relate to social ministry.
3. discusses principles of helping that grow out of basic Christian doctrines.
4. constructs a theology for helping.

Henlee H. Barnette correctly asserted that social ministry must be rooted in the character of God as revealed in Christ. He also stated that social ministry must be predicated on a biblical view of humanity.[1]

Any ministry of the church should be developed in harmony with the doctrine of God. This doctrine includes who God is, what God is like, what roles God plays in human lives, and how God wishes human beings to live. The doctrine of humanity is also important to consider when we design our programs of helping.

---

[1]Henlee H. Barnette, "Toward a Theological Basis for Social Work," *Western Recorder*, 12 December, 1957.

This doctrine includes what it means to be a human, humanity's need for God, how humans relate to God, and how humans relate to each other and to society.

Redemption is another theological issue important to social ministry. Questions such as the following need to be answered: What is the role of the social minister in the redemptive purpose of God and the church? What is the role of evangelism in social ministry? How does social ministry relate to evangelism? William Hendricks stated that the theological basis for Christian social ministries should be true of all our relationships: grateful obedience. As human beings, we can have no higher goal than sharing the love of God as expressed in the compassionate ministry and the suffering of God's Son, Jesus Christ.[2]

Theological principles related to the methods and techniques of helping are basic considerations in social ministry. Doctrinal issues related to the choice of methods and the techniques used to employ them will be discussed in this chapter.

The Doctrine of God

Who Is God?

The first response to this question must be that *He is.* Believing that God exists is crucial to the discussion of who God is: "anyone who comes to Him must believe that He exists" (Heb. 11:6). Many professional social workers and counselors have difficulty with the concept of God. They seem to feel that to acknowledge the reality of God would somehow reduce their stature as professionals. To them, scientifically generated knowledge seems more important than belief in a God who cannot be proven to exist by scientific methods. The fact that the nonexistence of God cannot be proven either sets up a stressful situation for honest professionals. Therefore, many choose to ignore discussions about God and leave Him out of their practice altogether.

If God is injected into the helping situation by the client system, the unbelieving or doubting professional may perceive the client's belief in God as a symptom of abnormality and try to extinguish the client's beliefs. Other professionals may simply ignore the client's religion. This could be unfortunate because if the client feels the subject is important enough to discuss with the

[2]William L. Hendricks, "A Theological Basis for Christian Social Ministries," *Review and Expositor* 85 (Spring 1988), 223.

worker, they should deal with the issue. To ignore it could hinder the successful resolution of a significant problem. Some emotionally disturbed persons develop what is called *religiosity*. This is a condition in which the person uses a distorted belief in God and religious teachings to cover some unhealthy attitude or explain a dysfunctional behavior. A helper with a good background in theology could be very useful in understanding and ministering to this type of client system.

> A group of social work students from a Christian college were visiting in a mental hospital. As they were walking past a large day room, a patient began to shout that God was angry and that he was going to destroy all of the people in the hospital. He became more and more agitated.

> One of the students walked over to the patient and said, "Sir, the God I know always cares for those He created. He does not want to harm you, no matter what you may have done. He loves you." The patient stopped his shouting and looked at the student for a moment before retreating to a couch where he sat looking out the window as though contemplating what the student had said.

> The psychiatrist who was guiding the tour was amazed. He stated that this was the first time he had seen the man calm down without medication.

From time to time, Christians who are professional social workers struggle with whether to allow their belief in God to color or shape their practice. They may be inclined to segment or compartmentalize their religious beliefs and their theories of professional practice. On Sundays (and other times) they may be active in leading Bible study and worship. At the office or in the professional community, they do not allow their religion to affect their behavior. They are sometimes troubled by persons who insist upon "talking religion" and "moralizing" with their clients.

Most evangelical Christians who are also human service professionals are aware that Christian doctrine teaches that Christianity is involved in every facet of the Christian's life. This would include one's professional life. How to accomplish this integration without violating one's professional integrity becomes an important question. In the same way, a social minister's concept of God is crucial to how he/she integrates beliefs with practice.

Who or what God is. For secular behavioral scientists, God is not a person. God is an abreaction in the mind of the believer. Some hypothesize that weak individuals construct a powerful being (God) who helps them to explain phenomena beyond their control or understanding. If secularists accept the concept at all, God is usually an abstraction beyond the understanding of mere human beings. They sometimes believe that a person who speaks of having a personal relationship with God or talking with God is delusional and shows symptoms of abnormal thinking and behaving.

Most professional social workers, psychologists, counselors, and psychiatrists were trained in schools that taught the theories of human behavior developed by secular behavioral scientists. It is therefore understandable that these professionals would have some difficulty integrating Christian beliefs about God with their practice theories. However, the Christian social minister seeks to accomplish just such an integration. For the Christian social minister, God is a person, not an idea or abstraction. It is therefore possible and desirable to establish and maintain an intimate relationship with God.

Since the issue is who God is, perhaps it would be best to begin with what God says about himself. In Exodus 3 we have the incident of the burning bush in which God tells Moses that His name is *Yahweh*, which is from the Hebrew root word meaning *to be*. God instructed Moses to tell Israel that "I Am" had sent him (Ex. 3:14). In other words, God is a being and the source of being.[3] For the social minister, this declaration is of utmost importance for two distinct reasons. (1) One's own personal faith is at stake. One cannot honestly represent a program built on belief in a being that he himself has not accepted. (2) The fact that God exists will be of great worth in the process of helping persons who have no hope and see no purpose in life. A belief in God provides purpose because God exists and cares about human beings. There can be more to the human's existence than the proverbial "rat race."

Who God is not. He is not a doting, bewhiskered grandfather. Although we call Him "Father," which implies a very familiar relationship, we must think of God in a more realistic way. He is our holy Parent and our extended suprafamily system. In this sense, He is the ultimate parent who chastises us, protects us, nurtures us, and serves as the source of our identity. We are called by His name

---

[3]R. L. Harris, G. L. Archer, and B. K. Waltke, eds., *Theological Wordbook of the Old Testament* (Chicago: Moody Press, 1980), 214.

(2 Chron. 7:14). He is the source of our comfort. We turn to Him in times of need, and He sustains us. He teaches us and guides us by His wise discipline (see Heb. 12:5-9).

God is an absolute judge, but his judgment is always merciful as well as just. While there is nothing hidden from Him, His surveillance is for our protection and His discipline for our good. His judgment is always administered in the context of His limitless and matchless love.

In *Your God Is Too Small,* J. B. Phillips has given us an excellent discussion of a number of "unreal gods" that seem to have power among Christians.[4] These "unreal gods" limit the "real" God's power in our lives, and they are essentially inoperative. Some of these unreal gods are the Resident Policeman, the Parental Hangover, the Grand Old Man, the Meek-and-Mild, the Absolute Perfection, the Heavenly Bosom, the God-in-a-Box, the Managing Director, the Second Hand, the Perennial Grievance, and the Pale Galilean. These are all inadequate descriptions of God. Although these concepts of God may have some measure of truth in them, they are all found lacking when describing the true personality of God.

God as a person. God acts, speaks, knows, wills, and decides. He can be angry, compassionate, jealous, and merciful. He is not a something; He is someone.[5] Actually, God is the only being who has perfect self-consciousness. His personality is eternally complete. He is completely self-determining—that is, He depends on nothing outside Himself for what He is or what He does.[6]

The God who has personality and who can be related to as "Our Father" is also the one who is in heaven (Matt. 6:9-13). This means that He is greater than humanity's limitations. Our knowledge of Him is incomplete unless we understand this.

When we speak of God we are limited to anthropomorphic language. Nothing we know of God can be communicated in any other way. We only know Him in terms of our own experience and therefore must be cautious not to attempt to make God in our image. We are made in the image of God. The original model is God Himself. If we wish to be real, genuine persons, we have but to

[4]J. B. Phillips, *Your God Is Too Small* (New York: Macmillan Company, 1962), 11-54.

[5]Shirley C. Guthrie, *Christian Doctrine* (Richmond: Covenant Life Curriculum Press, 1968), 109.

[6]Walter Thomas Conner, *Christian Doctrine* (Nashville: Broadman Press, 1937), 76.

learn how God lives and acts in a personal way.[7] Personality in God is necessary to account for personality in humans. As Conner declared, "Sin is against a person. Prayer is communion with a person. Religion is only a superstition and a sham if God is not a person."[8] When the social minister works with a person in need, he can do so in light of a God who is personal and is touched by the person's dilemma.

God is Spirit. The very essence of God's being is Spirit. As Spirit He transcends matter and is not bound by it. Humans are instructed to relate to Him as Spirit (John 4:24) and not to limit Him to images or material things. We are to think of Him in terms of mental and moral energy and life. The essence of God's being is Spirit, and the form it takes is personal. We relate to Him in faith and experience Him as an invisible spiritual power operative within us.[9] Through the witness of the Holy Spirit, we can be constantly aware of the eternal presence of God. We can also know that He is with those for whom we have responsibility. God can relate to both the helper and the one being helped in ways not limited by time, space, and material resources.

God is righteous. Three aspects of God's righteousness are important to a theology for social ministry in the church: (1) faithfulness—He is always on the side of right and truth, (2) purity—He is absolutely pure and there is no fault or defect in Him; the standard by which righteousness is measured is God, and (3) justice—He judges all equitably, without partiality, prejudice, or fault.[10] He is not sometimes loving and sometimes just; He is always both.

God's righteousness means that He is unconditionally and passionately on the side of the weak, the poor, the threatened, the oppressed, and the defenseless. He is for the lowly who were denied or deprived of their rights and against the proud, comfortable, and secure who hold their positions and possessions at the expense of others (see the Book of Amos). In being true to us, He remains true to Himself. He does not wink at our disobedience or good-naturedly shrug off our hurting of other people. He loves them as much as He loves us, and He is not pleased when we are disrespectful to any person. He is concerned about our guilt and injustice. He exercises His justice, lets His wrath burn, and punishes because He loves (Heb. 12:3-14). He judges and punishes in

---

[7]Guthrie, *Christian Doctrine*, 110.
[8]Conner, *Christian Doctrine*, 77-78.
[9]Ibid.
[10]Harold W. Tribble, *Our Doctrines* (Nashville: Broadman Press, 1936), 15.

order to bring us back to Himself and thus back to our own true selves.[11]

God is love. Abiding love is perhaps the most dramatic quality describing our personal experience with God. He is not sometimes loving and sometimes unloving. He does not love some people and hate others. He is loving in everything He does, always. Love is His nature (1 John 4:16). His is universal, unconditional, initiating love. God does not take back His love. It is reconciling love—costly, self-giving, helping, and renewing. He accepts persons as they are and frees those who will let Him, from their self-destroying rebellion against Him. He sets them on their own feet.[12] God will continue to love the sinner, even if the sinner chooses to reject Him.

The Primary Attributes of God

Omnipotence

God is absolute in power. This statement carries with it the idea that God is not dependent on anything outside Himself for His own existence. He is the source of all things. He is the fountain of all life.[13] He is all-powerful and is not limited by anything outside Himself. What God does and what He wills to do are always consistent with His nature. He can accomplish His will in weakness as well as strength, in defeat as well as victory, as a servant as well as the King of kings and Lord of lords.[14] What appears to humans as weakness God can use to accomplish His purpose. God can turn into a great victory what looks like defeat to the carnal world. For example, to the human observer, Christ's death on the cross was a defeat. God turned the cross into one of the most powerful symbols of all time. The social minister would do well to learn this lesson. When offered to God, what may appear to be weakness and defeat can be turned into strength and victory.

From this source we have our commission to minister. When Jesus gave the Great Commission He said, "All power [authority] is given unto me in heaven and in earth" (Matt. 28:18, KJV). Therefore, he sent us to minister to every person. That ministry includes the complete range of human needs. We are His instruments of help and the conductors of His power. Social ministers do not min-

[11]Guthrie, *Christian Doctrine*, 116-119.
[12]Ibid., 114-115.
[13]Conner, *Christian Doctrine*, 81.
[14]Guthrie, *Christian Doctrine*, 121.

ister by their own volition. Nor do they minister in their own strength.

Omnipresence

God is not limited by space. This means that he is immanent in the temporal order at all points of time and space. He is not present everywhere in the same sense with reference to the same end or purpose. His purpose in one case may be to sustain the natural order as natural, and in another instance to regenerate and sanctify.[15]

The concept of the omnipresence of God carries with it a consciousness of the present, the past, and the future. God is eternal, but He is always conscious of the historical moment as it relates to His creation. He is the God of the now and can be approached as present anywhere at any time. However, He is not limited by time and space and our deadlines. He is present and at work with the good and the bad of all races, all socioeconomic groups, all social classes, and each level of civilization. There is no place—not even hell—where God does not make His presence known in both His sovereignty and His love.[16]

No person or situation that the social minister will ever encounter has escaped the presence of God. God was there before the helper arrived. He will be there with the helper, and God will be there when the social minister has gone.

Omniscience

God has perfect knowledge. He knows everything that is an object of knowledge. God's knowledge is not limited by space, time, or events. He does not gain His knowledge from cause-effect relationships. He foreknew and designed everything. He foreknows the free acts of persons and it is God's will that they be free. God knows the events of the world order, not simply as isolated or detached events but as a part of the overall scheme of things. Every form of truth and every order of intelligence is grounded in the rational will of God.[17]

God has perfect knowledge and perfect wisdom. He has promised to give wisdom to us as we need it. The helper is always aware of the need to have as much information as possible for making right decisions when dealing with another person's life. When

---

[15]Conner, *Christian Doctrine*, 85.

[16]Guthrie, *Christian Doctrine*, 121-122.

[17]Conner, *Christian Doctrine*, 86-88.

that knowledge and wisdom is grounded in the One who knows all about human beings the minister is better equipped to make those decisions. God knows what is in the heart of every person. He provides insights and wisdom to the social minister (Jas. 1:5).

The Trinity

The unity of God denotes that there is only one God. Indeed, there can be only one self-existent, absolute being. Both the Old and New Testaments reveal the concept of God as monotheistic. There are not three Gods: there is only one. He is manifested in three ways and it takes all three personalities—Father, Son, and Holy Spirit—to complete the personality of God. To know God the Father is to know the Creator, the Sustainer, the all-powerful, all-knowing, always present God who loved the world so much that He gave His only Son to reconcile the world unto Himself. We see the righteous and just God who is also the redeeming God: the God in heaven who is also our Father.[18]

To know Christ the Son is to know God Himself. He was not just a man sent from God, a prophet, or an angel. He is God. Although He was born as a human, He was and is God. If we wish to know what God is like and who He is, we have only to look at Jesus. He was God made flesh dwelling among us.[19]

The Holy Spirit is the presence of God among all His creation. He is the Comforter, the ever-present help in time of trouble, the giver of gifts, the continuing presence of God working through His people, empowering their witness. He woos and convicts of sin, righteousness, and judgment. His presence with the social minister will guide him or her into all truth, comfort the minister and his or her client, and sustain them both according to the will of God working in them by the Holy Spirit (John 14:15-21; 16:7-11).

The God we serve is the basis of all that has meaning for the minister. Helping persons in trouble is in keeping with the very nature of God, and the doctrine of the triune God is in fact essential to this process. The power of God the Father, working through the model and work of His Son and through the continuing guidance and leadership of the Holy Spirit, provides the power by which human helping can be accomplished. This does not say that those who do not recognize the presence of God do not help effectively— quite the contrary. God is at work with the just and the unjust alike.

---

[18]Ibid., 82.
[19]Guthrie, *Christian Doctrine*, 95.

However, the helper who recognizes and uses knowledge of and commitment to God according to God's purpose will have a more adequate process by which to help.

The Doctrine of Humanity

When God became human He entered into history in a unique way. In so doing, He revealed much about Himself that we may come to know. However, He revealed much more about who we are. Through our faith in Christ we have a dimension of self-understanding that we can find nowhere else. This does not preclude our looking to the behavioral sciences and to philosophy for self-understanding, but these are incomplete without the revelation of God in Christ.

Humans are made in the image of God, not God in human image. The shape of the human body is probably not exactly like God's, but human spirit, personality, soul, and mental, emotional, and moral qualities are made in His image.

The Bible does not dissect the human into body, mind, and spirit. Some speak of a person as soul, spirit, and body. This is essentially a Greek idea. The biblical view of the human is that of a whole. One does not have a soul; he or she is a soul (Gen. 2:7). Guthrie stated that in the Bible, the human is not essentially spiritual or physical. Humanity has to do with a whole being—spiritual and physical, soul and body—not with just a part.[20]

According to the Bible, the human is the "image of the invisible God" (Col. 1:15, KJV), was made in "the form of God" (Phil. 2:6, KJV). Jesus was the ideal human. He lived completely for God and in complete obedience to God. He also loved others completely and lived in complete identity with them. He taught us that to be truly human, to be made in the image of God, is more than to possess intellectual, spiritual, or moral qualities; it is to be person-in-encounter.[21] This means that we are intimately involved with other persons. We are aware that what happens to "the least of these" is of concern to God and to us (Matt. 25:40).

Humanity's Relationship with God

Humanity was created in the image of God for fellowship with God (Gen. 1:26-27; 2:15-25). Something in the human is always

---

[20]Ibid., 190.
[21]Ibid., 193.

incomplete when the relationship with God is strained or severed. In fact, one of the primary meanings of death is separation from the presence of God. Humans find their ultimate meaning, purpose, and completeness in God. A human without God will be continually dissatisfied with life and incomplete in all relationships.

Total dependence is the phrase that best describes humanity's basic relationship with God. God is the author and finisher of faith and existence. Without God, human existence has no meaning. There is no purpose in life. Everything humanity has and is comes from God and is sustained by God.[22]

Human Relationships

God's revealed will is for humanity's ultimate good. Nothing will be required that is not ultimately for the human's own benefit and according to God's design. The human being will find happiness in nothing else. This purpose is summed up in the law stating that we are to love God with everything we are—and, in order to carry out God's purpose, to love others as ourselves (see. Matt. 22:34-40; Mark 12:28-34; Luke 10:25-37).

We serve God by serving each other. As the instruments of His love we are to relate to others the way God has taught us through the life and work of Jesus. We need each other. We cannot escape our social environment. We may be able to isolate ourselves from part of our social environment, but we will only be successful in reducing its parameters.[23]

Human relationships are consistent with God's primary design. Fellowship is a primary quality of the human relationship. Those who need our help provide us an opportunity to be of service to God by allowing us to help them. When we need help, we allow our brothers and sisters to gain the blessing of God by asking them to help us.

Our relationships with others are to be nonjudgmental, like God's. He is no respecter of persons. Even His enemies enjoy the blessings of His grace. He causes the rain to rain on the just and the unjust alike. The sun shines upon the wicked as well as the good. This is God's way, and the creature (human) is to follow the example of the Creator.

Our helping is not to be self-seeking. That is, we help because the other person needs help, not for what we can get out of it for

---

[22]Ibid., 194.
[23]Hendricks, "A Theological Basis for Christian Social Ministries," 223.

ourselves. There is nothing wrong with receiving praise from our peers, but to help in order to gain praise is foreign to a Christlike attitude.

In our relationships with other persons we recognize not only that God created all persons with a common humanity, but also that He created them as unique individuals. Because of the individuality of persons, God does not treat everyone alike. However, because of the common humanity we share, He did many things that are universal in scope. Christ's death on the cross was both universal and personal. It was universal in that He died for all. It was individual in that each person must respond individually to Christ's claims on his or her life.

Jesus totally committed himself to other persons, yet He never lost His identity. He fulfilled His primary task by uncompromisingly sticking to it. We can fulfill our human tasks by recognizing our debt to all persons. At the same time, we find and assert who we are in light of what God intended us to be.[24]

The Doctrine of Sin and Redemption

Sinning is deliberately rebelling against God's will and purpose. It is missing the mark. It is giving in to fleshly desires. It is violating the integrity of other persons. It is refusing to do good when we know to do good. It is doing wrong deliberately. It is rebelling against God and His purpose for our lives. It is disobeying Jesus' primary directive to love God and neighbor.

Ultimately, sin is a general state of being that is not in harmony with God's purpose. It is not necessary to name specific sins because the very nature of each act of omission or commission will be judged in light of God's love as it is manifested in us. Any behavior that ignores God is sin. In the same manner, anything we do that does not contribute to the well-being of another person is sin. Anything we do not do when we have opportunity that would help another person is sin. In other words, sin is willfully departing from what we know to be the right behaviors. As willful sinners we deny our best impulse—communion with God—and choose the paths of selfishness and greed.

Anthropological pessimism, which sees no hope for humanity, is not consistent with Christian theology. Neither is anthropological optimism, which postulates that humans lack only

---

[24]Guthrie, *Christian Doctrine*, 201.

CHRISTIAN SOCIAL MINISTRY

education or opportunity to make them good, consistent with a realistic view of humanity. However, a balance of both optimism and pessimism may provide the basis for a realistic view of human nature. This view in turn provides an adequate rationale for social ministries.[25]

Redemption is the deliberate act of a gracious God, requiring only acceptance by persons who realize that life's ultimate questions cannot be realized without His help. God does not wait for humans to make the move toward Him. In fact, humanity is completely separated from God. Humans are incapable of overcoming sin and paying for it themselves. At this point the love of God overcomes sin and takes the initiative in redeeming humans from sin and ultimate destruction. Scripture informs us "that God was in Christ, reconciling the world unto himself" (2 Cor. 5:19, KJV). "God commendeth his love toward us, in that, while we were yet sinners, Christ died for us" (Rom. 5:8, KJV). The very purpose for which Jesus came to earth as a human being was to redeem us from our sin.

While the ultimate form of redemptive love was seen in Christ, God had been redeeming persons long before Christ. God initiated the covenants of the Old Testament for the purpose of redeeming humans.

According to Hendricks, the miracles of Christ were more than works of compassion. In addition, they were promises of what God will ultimately do for His people when His kingdom is fully come. He will remove pain, death, evil, and the limitations of the present human existence. The redemptive work of God is still going on in this world through the auspices of His people.[26]

Because of God's work through Christ in redemption, all that God asks of the human is deliberate repentance and faith. This decision is reasoned, logical, and emotional. It is a reasoned decision because God's demand for repentance presupposes His mercy, love, and forgiveness. By repenting, the sinner lays hold of a salvation which is not simply "reserved" for him, but which in fact is constantly extended to him.[27] It is an emotional decision because persons are moved to action by emotions. Logic alone will not bring about change. Action must be taken, and the emotions enable the volition of human beings.

---

[25]Hendricks, "A Theological Basis for Christian Social Ministries," 223-231.

[26]William L. Hendricks, "The Theology of the New Testament," *Broadman Bible Commentary,* Vol. 8 (Nashville: Broadman Press, 1969), 35.

[27]Victor P. Furnish, *The Love Commandment* (Nashville: Abingdon Press, 1972), 58.

The social minister encounters people who have no hope. Often they feel that they have somehow committed the unpardonable sin against God and against society. The redemptive purpose of God can be carried out by enabling these persons to know His forgiveness.

A minister and a psychiatrist both served on the board of a mental health association. They often drove to the meetings together. One night, after attending a board meeting, the psychiatrist said to the minister, "You ministers have the best of both worlds. You not only possess the skills of counseling, but you can also offer your clients forgiveness. We psychiatrists can't do that. Forgiveness is one thing that 95 percent of my patients need." The psychiatrist was unwilling to discuss his own personal faith. He indicated that he just could not believe "that stuff."

Enabling persons to know the complete forgiveness that comes with repentance and conversion, making Jesus Christ Lord and Savior, is one of the most important assets the Christian social minister brings to the helping situation. At this point the social minister assumes the role of evangelist.

International Principles for Helping

Hendricks stated that a Christian theological understanding of the method of social ministry is incarnation. Desiring to help persons in stress is consistent with God's purpose and plan. The nature and activity of God is revealed in Jesus Christ as an expression of love, compassion, and sacrificial service. Christian social ministers should remember that all ministry, Christ's and ours, requires embodiment and action. The incarnation provides motive, motif, and mode for the Christian social minister.[28]

First Principle: Concern for Persons

Working with individuals, one to one, is basic to the way God deals with humanity. God is concerned about the world and all persons in it. His concern has global applications, but He also recognizes the uniqueness of each individual. His work is primarily with individual persons. In Matthew 25:1-46, we have the account of the judgment of the nations. The judgment is global, but the criterion is personal: "Whatever you did for one of the least of these... you did for me" (v. 40).

---

[28]Hendricks, "A Theological Basis for Christian Social Ministires," 226.

Second Principle: Action

God always acts concretely with a specific person at a definite time, in a particular place, to meet immediate personal needs and to meet the person's ultimate need of redemption. Ministry does not take place unless all three dimensions are present and operative. One is not ministering if the act of helping does not occur with a specific person at a definite time in a particular place.

Third Principle: The Significance of All Persons

All human beings are created in the image of God, and all are of value and worth to God. Helping can only be done in light of the worth of the person being helped. Every individual is significant, no matter who he is, how she looks, where he came from, or what she has done.

Fourth Principle: God as Primary Resource

God is the sustainer of all life, and He is the primary resource for the helper and the person being helped. However, this does not mean that persons should just sit around and let God fill their mouths, provide the money, and so on. The God who owns the cattle on thousands of hills and all the gold and silver has ordained that humans are to use appropriate methods of acquiring and appropriating these resources.

God's primary resource for helping one in need is the helper. God has chosen to use human instruments to help other human beings. He will always be operative in the process. The Holy Spirit will be present with the helper and the one being helped. He will be a part of any process of interaction that leads to helping.

If helpers are to be consistent as God's resources, they must make wise use of God's Word, the Bible. The Scriptures have the power to transform both ministers' and clients' standing with God (justification). The Scriptures also have the power to transform persons' condition or state of being (sanctification). The Word of God is the source of all godliness, and it has the power to produce faith, even in persons who have difficulty believing. Social ministers who use the Scriptures wisely have access to the dynamic power of God to change persons' lives.[29]

---

[29]Jay Adams, *A Theology of Christian Counseling* (Grand Rapids: Zondervan Publishing Company, 1986), 34-37.

Fifth Principle: Self-determination

God has given us free will and He does not violate that gift. Persons can even choose to reject God. Although the person will suffer the predetermined consequences for such choices, God does not override the person's will. The helper must not violate that principle in working with individuals or groups. This does not mean that the social minister must submit to every whim of the one being helped, but the minister must recognize the right of the person to refuse the type of service offered. The minister respects the client's right to decide which needs he or she wishes to do something about.

Sixth Principle: Patience

Growing out of our recognition of the right of the person to self-determination is our remembrance of God's long-suffering and patience. The Holy Spirit gently convicts and woos the wayward child of God, often over long periods of time, before any positive moves are made. The helper must also be patient in order to enable persons to overcome inhibitions regarding help and to begin taking positive steps toward self-reliance and personal fulfillment.

Seventh Principle: Personal Responsibility

While it is within the capacity of God to do everything for humans—to make all decisions, protect persons from the consequences of their choices, and guide them around dangers—He chooses not to do so. Along with the freedom of choice God gives to humanity, God has also provided for a day of judgment. At this judgment every person will be held accountable for the choices he has made and the actions she has taken.

The earth was cursed for Adam's sake when he was driven from the garden of Eden as a consequence of his disobedience of God's command (Gen. 3:17). In His wisdom God does not interfere with the natural consequences of a person's behavior. He expects persons to learn to do all that He has created them to do for themselves. Persons are not to be totally reliant upon others.

While we recognize that we are totally dependent upon God, even for the air we breathe, we are to carry out His will in doing all that He has equipped us to do according to His purpose. He gave us minds and bodies with which to function in the world. Therefore, we function at our best when we use all these abilities according to His purpose. Helpers who do everything for their clients and make all their decisions for them are not helping. The client's dignity and integrity are being violated.

Summary and Conclusions

God's power is available to the helper who is working according to God's plan. Social ministers look at individuals through the eyes of Christ and seek to minister without regard to class structure, race, ethnic origin or any other classification. All persons are equal in the sight of God and need to be viewed in the same way by social ministers.[30]

Jesus said, "All power is given unto me" (Matt. 28:18, KJV); therefore, He sent social ministers, in light of that power, knowing that the Holy Spirit would work through them and that He would be with them, even to the end of the world. At that point salvation will be complete and Christ will rule all persons and all things eternally.

Thus social ministers look back to see how God has worked with humanity in the past in order to understand the redemptive purpose of God in working with persons today. They look up to God who transcends the limitations of this present and confused generation, and look inward to realize the presence of the loving Father who enables, empowers, enlightens, and gives direction to present-day helping.

Our helping is eschatological in that it looks forward to the coming of the kingdom of God in its fullness, when our salvation is complete. This message provides a firm foundation upon which to build a personal ministry with persons both inside and outside the community of faith. It provides hope for the hopeless, helpless, and powerless who are loved by God and by the Christian, who by identification is a helper. It tells us that God has no intention of saving humans without also saving their environment. God is working in society through Christian people to accomplish His will and redemptive purpose. He is working in society even beyond the knowledge of Christian people in order to accomplish His eschatological purpose.

Exercises for Review and Examination

1. List and discuss each of the titles for who God is.

---

[30]Ronald W. Loftis, *Church and Community Ministries Director's Manual* (Atlanta: Home Mission Board, 1987), vi.

2. Discuss the concept of God as person.

3. Discuss the righteousness of God as it relates to the fact that God is love.

4. List and describe the role of the attributes of God in personal helping.

5. Discuss the meaning of the description "made in the image of God."

6. Write a one-page discussion of the place of the doctrine of redemption in personal helping.

7. List and define seven principles of helping that grow out of a theological base.

8. Write a paper of five pages or more on the subject "My Theology of Helping."

Chapter Five

Philosophical Foundations for Christian Social Ministry

Goal: A study of this chapter should enable the social minister to understand ways in which congregations, denominational judicatories, and church-related agencies conceptualize social ministry.

Objectives: The minister . . .

1. defines the term *social ministry*.
2. relates social ministry to other functions of the church.
3. delineates principles of social ministry.
4. discusses the qualities of the social minister.
5. describes obstacles that cause persons to need help.
6. formulates a philosophy of social ministry.

Social Ministry

The term *social* speaks of relationships primarily between human beings. All persons are undeniably involved with all other persons. Each birth adds to us. Each death diminishes us. When others grieve or experience sorrow, we feel with them (some more than others). We are affected when persons whom we know suffer emotionally. When relationship problems arise in other families or in communities, we are more ill at ease in our personal relationships. By God's design we are all involved in humanity. God is involved, and He not only inspires our involvement but He commands it.

The term *ministry* is not always easy to define specifically. It can refer to a governmental office such as the Ministry of Finance. Churches often use it to designate the function in a particular area of church life, such as the pastoral ministry, the educational ministry, or the outreach ministry. As noted in the Introduction, we are using the term *ministry* synonymously with *help*. As such, it denotes a process in contrast to a specific office. All of the offices of the church involve helping (ministry) or service as a part of their function.

Social ministry is an organized process used by redeemed individuals called by God to proclaim the good news, to demonstrate Christ's concern for the spiritual, physical, emotional, mental, and relational well-being of persons, families, and groups both inside and outside the community of faith.

Social Ministry and Church Functions

Because the ministry function is the purview of every Christian, it seems appropriate to locate it in the overall functional schema of the church. Four major functions (or functional areas) have been identified: worship, proclaim and witness, nurture and educate, and minister.[1] Each of these overlaps. There is, for example, an educational, proclaiming, and ministry function in worship. Persons who attend worship services are often in need of a word from the Lord that speaks to their needs and helps them to make it through another week. Much of the theology that persons assimilate comes from the hymns used in worship. Sermons should be educational. Preaching, singing, praying, and Bible reading are important tools used in proclamation and witness, leading persons to accept Jesus Christ as Lord and Savior.

Worship, proclamation and witness, and ministry are involved in education. When persons meet for Bible study, discipleship training, and missions education, there is often an evangelistic outcome. Sunday School classes become social and emotional support groups. Classes are often called upon to help persons with physical needs as well as spiritual needs. Worship through Bible reading, prayer, and song is often part of the agenda for the various educational programs of the church.

[1]Robert A. Orr, *Being God's People* (Nashville: Convention Press, 1987), 44-47.

Proclamation and witness have worship, ministry, and educational functions. To present the claims of the gospel to persons who are not Christians, a church most often uses Bible reading and testimony—worship functions. The ultimate need of every dysfunctional person is to have a personal relationship with Jesus Christ as Lord and Savior. In this sense, proclamation and witness is ministry. There is a definite educational function in witnessing to persons who do not know Christ. They must come to know, understand, and apply the gospel to their lives. Those are all educational terms.

The ministry of the church is a totality (see the diagram). Each of the four frames interact to form the whole. A healthy church achieves a dynamic balance among these functions.

WORSHIP	WITNESS AND PROCLAIM
MINISTER	NURTURE AND EDUCATE

To minister is to meet the total needs of persons in Jesus' name.[2] This is the responsibility of every Christian in the church. Some ministries will be performed spontaneously by members as they relate to neighbors, friends, and other acquaintances. However, just as there is a need for organized Bible study, training, outreach, and worship, there is a need for an organized ministry of helping. The needs of persons should be met within the purview of each major functional area of the church.

Principles of Social Ministry

Growing out of what we have come to realize is the nature of God and His involvement with humanity, we can deduce seven basic principles.

---

[2]Harold K. Graves, *The Nature and Functions of a Church* (Nashville: Convention Press, 1963), 123.

First Principle: Social Ministry Is Rooted and Grounded in God's Love for all Persons.

This love is unselfish, self-giving, unconditional, rational, all-inclusive, and ultimately concerned for the well-being of its object. The principle of unselfish and self-giving love highlights the difference between helping programs designed with ulterior motives in mind and those based upon God's love. Church programs of helping are often used as "bait" for adding members to the organization or to "inflate" the baptismal record. It is true that each of the numbers added to the record represent persons, and it is also true that God has concern for every person. Even so, using ministry programs as "bait" is unethical and contrary to God's revelation. If the church is self-giving in its outreach rather than self-seeking, the result will likely be additions to the fellowship. This should be a natural *result* rather than a *motive* for ministry.

The first and primary concern of our ministry is the well-being of the persons we encounter. If persons need clothing, we clothe them. If persons need food, we feed them. If persons need housing, we help them find shelter. If persons do not know Jesus Christ as Savior, we attempt to lead them to Christ. We do not do the first in order to do the last; we do *all* these things because we are concerned for every person's total well-being.

God's love is unconditional. Anyone may come to Him and receive life everlasting. When our ministry programs follow God's example, they will have the same unconditional quality. We will not exclude any person for whom Jesus died. God is in the business of including people in His redemptive plan, and He requires His churches to do the same in *all* their functions.

God's love is rational. It is not a sentimental love. Our helping will also have this quality when we follow His example. We need to use a reasoned process when we consider a request for help. We want to make judgments that are both rational and caring. This is what the Scriptures mean when they speak of wisdom. God promised in His Word to give us wisdom if we ask for it.

Second Principle: Social Ministry Recognizes and Supports the Worth, Dignity and Integrity of the Individual.

It is unthinkable that, in the name of the One who gave humans worth by dying for them, any person could be considered unworthy of our help. However, many Christians have been guilty of judging the worth of persons. They designate some "worthy" and some "unworthy." Some persons are considered "unworthy" because they appear to be professional "beggars." They rarely tell the truth about their situation.

> A woman drove up outside a church in an old, beat-up station wagon full of rowdy, dirty children. She brought the youngest one in with her while she made her request for assistance. She said that she was out of food, and she had seven children and a sick husband to feed. She also needed some money to pay the rent or the landlord would throw her and her children out in the street along with her sick husband. She could also use some help in purchasing medicine for her disabled husband.

> It was the policy of the church to gather basic social information on every person requesting help. Her address was near a large church which had an active social ministry program. The social minister called the church and found that the woman had already been there that day and carried away a full month's supply of groceries. She had also gathered several items of clothing for each person in her family. The church was looking into the rent and medical situation.

> A further check revealed that the welfare department was also involved in helping with the rent money and medical bills. The welfare caseworker told the social minister that this was a pattern with this woman. She usually "made" four or five churches each month. The welfare caseworker told the social minister that the woman would often sell the clothing and the canned goods in order to buy liquor for herself and her alcoholic husband.

It is obvious that this woman was defrauding the churches in the city. She did not really need the help she was requesting; however, she did need help. By treating her as a person of worth, guarding her dignity, and respecting her integrity, the social minister possibly could help her with her actual needs. Doing so would involve a great deal of time, energy, and patience. Is she worth it? How about the children? She, the children and her husband are worth it!

Respecting persons' worth, integrity, and dignity means that we allow them the right to self-determination. They do not have to take the help we offer. They have the right to decide what needs they are willing to allow someone to help with. As persons of worth, they should be granted the same opportunities others enjoy, limited only by their own abilities.[3]

Third Principle: Social Ministry Offers the Kind of Help a Person Can Use to Improve His/Her Own Situation.

This principle recognizes the integrity of the individual and the creative quality God designed into every person. Persons must be allowed to participate in their own life decisions and to do what they can to care for themselves and their families. They also need to have an opportunity to make a contribution to their world.[4] Any process of helping that does not operationalize this principle will usually result in dependency. The result could be a lack of initiative and will to survive. The person we attempt to help may have been harmed rather than helped. The goal of help built upon this principle is self-support.

> Annie came to the church for some groceries one hot summer afternoon in early August. She had been crying all day. Sam, the man she was living with, had left her the day before, and she did not know where to find him. She had no place to turn. She said that if Sam did not return she was going to kill herself. She had nothing to eat in her dingy, one-room apartment. The social minister went with her to her apartment to help carry some groceries.

> In the meantime Sam had returned. He had been mugged in a downtown parking lot and left there all night. Obviously they both needed help. Instead of giving them money and supplying them with food indefinitely, the minister, with Sam's concurrence, began to help Sam find ways of earning money. The day-care center allowed Annie to work part-time in payment for groceries she received from the food closet.

> The social minister worked intensely with this couple for almost a year. Sam had held a job for four months, and it seemed that he would keep it this time. Annie had devel-

---

[3]Walter A. Friedlander, ed., *Concepts and Methods of Social Work* (Englewood Cliffs: Prentice-Hall, 1976), 1-9.
[4]Ibid., 6.

oped some personal pride and continued to work as a part-time helper in the day-care center. They were both active in attendance at a local mission.

This kind of help went beyond the material; it was useful in meeting the actual needs of this couple.[5]

Fourth Principle: Social Ministry Shows Concern for the Whole Person.

We are told to love God and our neighbor with all our soul, heart, mind, and strength (Matt. 22:37; Mark 12:30; Luke 10:27). This actually represents the totality of our being, and these qualities represent the basic domains of living. We should be conscious of the status of functioning in each domain of the client's life. When we help in one area, stress often appears in another. If we intervene at the right point, we may alleviate stress in other areas of a person's life.

> Manuel was a hard worker and had a good work record. However, there were no jobs he could do unless he could read and write. He had a wife and two small children. He had often been told that if he would learn to read and write English, he could be put to work immediately.
>
> He came to the Ministry Center for help, having been told that a literacy program was operating there. The social minister called several persons to inquire about the possibility of a job for Manuel while he was studying English. Even a part-time job would benefit Manuel greatly. The social minister contacted the Department of Human Resources about a training grant for Manuel. It seemed reasonable to the agency and the employees that if Manuel could just hold out he would learn to read and write and then could get a good job.
>
> The social minister recognized that his family had to eat and have a place to live while Manuel was learning. By helping him with more than just his reading and writing, the social minister made it possible for all of Manuel's basic human needs to be met. Manuel was able to work part-time, study reading and writing at night, and use a training grant that enabled him to care for himself and his

---

[5]Alan Keith-Lucas, *Giving and Taking Help* (Chapel Hill: University of North Carolina Press, 1972), 3-19.

family. This enhanced his feelings of worth, restored his dignity, and allowed him to live with his family in his community with integrity.

Because of the Christlike work of this center, Manuel attended revival services and made a profession of faith some time later. He has not joined the church but continues to attend services regularly.

The concept of ministering to the whole person is evident in this case example.[6]

Fifth Principle: Social Ministry Is Committed to Quality Service.

There is no way that an imperfect person can offer a perfect sacrifice to God. However, God has provided that sacrifice for us. He always wants the best for His children, and He gave the best, providing a model for us. He asks no less than our best as we serve those whom He loves.

Often churches take on more than they can possibly do well. Resources are limited in most churches. By attempting to serve every person with every need, we spread our resources so thin that we do no real good. In other words, quality is sacrificed for quantity, and this is not in keeping with God's plan for our ministry. God expects us to use the resources He has provided. If He wants us to serve more persons, He will provide more resources. It is better for us to work with a few whom we can serve well than to take on more than we can possibly help.

An after-school Bible club program was started in a local housing project community center. A survey had revealed that there were over eight hundred children in the project. There were only six workers who could be counted on to staff the program.

The assistant director of the sponsoring mission center wanted the workers to take all the children they could pack into the rooms. However, the director insisted that the workers take only the number of children they could handle with some degree of efficiency and effectiveness. He wanted to stress a quality club program rather than one that overloaded the capacity of the three rooms avail-

---

[6]David O. Moberg, *Inasmuch* (Grand Rapids: Wm. B. Eerdmans Publishing Co., 1965), 13-27.

able and the workers' ability to do an effective job. The assistant director felt that there were many children who needed what the clubs could offer and that they would be taught something, which would be better than nothing, even though the conditions were not the best.

The reason the director insisted upon a quality program is directly related to the principle of quality service. It is better to do our work in the name of Christ well than to bring discredit to His name and His church by doing an ineffective job, trying to serve too many with too little. In the long run more people will get more real help, and our witness will be more effective in the community.[7] When the ministry program does not have the resources to meet all the identified needs, additional resources should be found. Sometimes this requires the ministry staff to do some networking with other service programs.

Providing quality service often means making use of available community resources, such as private and public social service agencies. We show poor stewardship of the resources God has entrusted to our care when we duplicate services already available. However, churches often refuse to use secular organizations. Some feel that these organizations are inadequate to deal with the problems, or they are afraid they will lose their clients to the "atheistic" welfare organizations. Of course, this logic does not stand up against the truth. Often the workers in these organizations are members of the very church that refused to refer to them. Sometimes distrust grows between these agencies and the churches because of a distrust of each others' philosophies or methods.

Just as every Christian has been endowed with special talents and abilities, churches are full of gifted persons with specific qualities that can be used in ministry. These persons can be enlisted to develop an exciting array of ministries. However, no one should try to do everything for every person in the community. Good stewardship requires that we do well what we can, use our resources wisely, and make effective use of the resources available to us in the community, for the sake of the client.

Bob W., a minister in a First Baptist Church in a town of ten thousand persons, came in contact with an elderly woman. She and her retarded son were living in a dingy, rat-infested, airy shack on the edge of town. The son had been sick and unable to work at the restaurant where he

---

[7]Moberg, *Inasmuch*, 103-122.

washed dishes on weekends. This job, plus his mother's Social Security check, provided just enough for them to get by each month.

After Bob visited the home he began to put together a list of needs he had observed. The church could not meet all of these needs. He called the mission action leader who rounded up some warm clothing for the woman and her son. He called an apartment owner and arranged for the family to move in without the customary deposit at a rent they were able to pay.

He called the First Methodist Church and arranged for them to gather some basic furniture. An appliance store loaned them a used stove and refrigerator until they could make payments on them. A couple of men volunteered to use their pickup trucks to help them move.

The minister discovered that the woman was not drawing the Social Security benefits she was entitled to and took her to the Social Security office. Her income was boosted to $350 per month from the $112 she had previously received. In addition, she would be eligible for Medicaid benefits.

Another church in town needed someone to help clean up and wash the dishes after the Wednesday evening church dinner, so they hired the son. This provided enough income to meet the basic needs of this family. The older ladies' Sunday School class was asked to visit the woman. Soon she was attending regularly.

Sixth Principle: Social Ministry Is a Primary Function of the Church.

Pinson reinforced the idea that ministry is a primary function of the church.[8] Just as the church is concerned with the worship, witness, and religious education of its members, there is a strong mandate from God's Word regarding ministry to the total needs of persons. This function is vitally involved in the will and purpose of God for His church.

In her book *Creative Social Ministry for the Church*, Melton stressed the primary role of social ministry in the life of the church.[9]

---

[8]William M. Pinson, *Applying the Gospel* (Nashville: Broadman Press, 1975), 15-39.
[9]Alpha Melton, *Creative Social Ministry for the Church* (Nashville: Broadman Press, 1970), 1-23.

Graves stated that the church should be aware of human need, and all Christians should be involved. The church is responsible for leading each member to find a place in ministry.[10] Howse and Thomason affirmed this principle by stating that the church exists for people—those who live without the Savior.[11]

The Bible says that God's people should be sensitive to ministry opportunities; it contains many specific illustrations about God's purpose and ministry. In fact, the Bible says much more about ministry to persons with social needs than about evangelism. The Bible does not make a distinction between the two. Evangelism is a ministry function. It must be assumed, therefore, that God intends helping ministries to have a prominent place in the church's program along with evangelism.

Seventh Principle: Social Ministry Is Aggressive.

As an outgrowth of God's love, social ministry is by nature aggressive. Social ministers are always looking for opportunities to reach out and serve. God seeks persons. He initiated the covenants of the Old Testament, and the New Testament is the product of His initiation. It is the nature of God to be actively involved with His creation. He does not force Himself on humans, but He initiates the contact. When we are aware of a another's need, it is our Christian responsibility to make our helping presence available in such a way that the person can receive it and use it. We are not to help only those who come knocking at our door. Our love for our neighbors should cause us to seek them out in their time of need and to make our resources available to them.

> Aunt Mary, an elderly lady, lived two blocks from a church at the edge of an inner-city neighborhood. She was a proud person and delighted in helping every person who came by her home as well as anyone in need in the neighborhood. She was always sharing from her beautiful garden and flower beds. Her house was always well kept, although it was a modest frame dwelling.
>
> One day a pastor drove by her home and noticed that weeds were taking over her garden and that the house was in ill repair. The steps to her porch were broken, and

---

[10]Graves, *The Nature and Functions of a Church*, 123-131.

[11]W. L. Howse and W. O. Thomason, *A Dynamic Church* (Nashville: Convention Press, 1962), 9.

the paint was peeling around the windowsills. Some screens were hanging loose. He spoke to the Brotherhood director about the situation and the two of them went to visit with Aunt Mary, even though she was not a member of the church. (She was an active member of another denomination.)

They discovered that she had had a serious illness during the winter and could not work on her garden or house as she once did. They offered to have the men and boys take on the project of cleaning her yard and garden and making some minor repairs on her house. She agreed to allow them to do so. The Baptist Men and RAs gathered for two Saturdays and completed the work.

This love in action was aggressive. It was a witness to the whole neighborhood, and respect for the church grew significantly among the people. That church became known as the church that cares. Although the community is changing, the church has grown while others are dying in similar neighborhoods. Because of aggressive ministry action, the membership is an excited community of faith.

Qualities of the Social Minister

When the process of social ministry is reduced to its lowest common denominator, the relationship between two human beings is where ministry actually takes place. Helping is an act, either tangible or intangible, offered by one person to another in such a way that the person can use it to achieve some sense of fulfillment.[12] Not every human relationship results in help. Some relationships cause harm, even when the helper has acquired a number of helping skills. There are certain qualities the social minister must possess in order to be effective:

1. *Warmth.* This quality refers to that part of one's personality identified with his humanness. The minister is able to display an attitude of friendliness, recognition of the other person's worth, and respect. The minister relates to the client as one human being to another. She cares about the well-being of the client.

2. *Empathy.* This means to feel with, to understand, not just intellectually but also emotionally. Empathy has an element of sympathy in it, but these terms are not synonymous. Sympathy refers

---

[12]Keith-Lucas, *Giving and Taking Help*, 15.

to feeling the same thing; it is identification. One who empathizes feels the hurt in the other person, understands, and cares that the person is hurting. Sympathy can get in the way of the social minister. It may cause the minister to suffer the same incapacitating qualities as the one needing help.

The empathetic helper can feel the discomfort of another, but is not waylaid by it. The minister may cry with the bereaved at the loss of a loved one, but the minister does not grieve with them at the same depth. The minister is not incapacitated by the other person's problems. The minister may feel the loneliness experienced by an older person living alone, but she is not lonely. The minister can realize that a person is hurting and understand that it is not pleasant, but he does not feel pressured to experience the same feeling in order to help.

3. *Authenticity.* In the common vernacular, the minister must be "real." People who are hurting can generally detect insincerity in a minister if they are around him long enough. "Gushing" and "cooing" are symptoms of insincerity, coming across as phony. The frozen smile is also a symptom of a phony. The grunts and groans of a nondirective counselor often come across as unreal. When a person is authentic, there is a natural warmth and empathy. The minister will not pretend warmth, friendliness, and caring.

Because the Holy Spirit dwells within the social minister, her caring has an authentic quality. The social minister can see value in persons because God loves them. Therefore, ministers can work for their client's well-being even if the client is hard to love.

Pitfalls of the Social Minister

There are some pitfalls or dangers social ministers must be aware of and guard against. Because social ministers are often given a great deal of power over their client, they must be careful about how that power is used. The following paragraphs, contain dangers social ministers should avoid.

The self-protection syndrome. Social ministers gain a great deal of satisfaction from seeing persons grow to stand on their own feet. However, this is not their motive for helping. The social minister's motive is the client's well-being. It is easy to fall into the trap where what is done has to please the minister. If it doesn't, the minister becomes dissatisfied with the client. This dissatisfaction becomes evident when the client does not demonstrate an expected rate of progress.

Some persons may enter helping professions for the purpose of resolving their own personal problems. They seem to feel that if they are helping someone else, their own problems will go away. These persons often see their problems in other people and become incapable of making adequate problem assessments. They will often project their own feelings to the client and will assume that their motives are the same as the client's. Persons may work in volunteer programs for the same reasons.

> A volunteer often complained that no one at her house ever seemed to notice what she did for them. Her husband was never at home, and the children were always going off and leaving her to the drudgery of the house. She had come to the center to volunteer her car and her time to transport mothers with small children to the outpatient clinic in another part of the city.

> She complained to the director that the people did not seem to appreciate what she was doing for them. Each week, as she transported persons to and from the clinic, she kept remarking about how grateful these women ought to be that someone like her would give her time and use her own car to take them places. The women expressed gratitude, but would not ride with her the next week. Soon no one from that community would ride with her.

The codependent rescuer syndrome. When ministers feel a compulsion to bail clients out of trouble, they are being codependent. By not allowing clients to fail, ministers are stripping them of their integrity. This behavior ultimately causes a strain on the helping relationship.

> Jack had been coming to church for some time when he met the minister after church one evening and asked him for a ride. He shared the fact that he had lost his driver's license and that he was going to be fired. He told the minister that he would have to move out of his apartment. He did not know where to go. The minister immediately went to work to find a solution to Jack's pressing problem. He called friends and got Jack several job interviews. Within a two-week period he had spent over twenty hours trying to rescue Jack from his situation.

Over the next three months Jack was hired and fired by several employers. He would not show up for work more than two days at a time, and he was often late when he did appear. Jack would walk off the job in anger and get fired again. Jack left town and the minister said it seemed that he was trying to get away. This assessment was probably correct.

The Messiah syndrome. Ministers who must sacrifice themselves for their clients suffer from this syndrome. They must do all things and be all things to their clients in order to save their poor clients from immediate destruction. The term *Messiah* is not used here in reference to Christ but to the attitude of ministers who do not realize their limitations. They must suffer for their clients and usually want everyone to know of their sacrifices. If others do not lift them up, they will lift themselves up so that all can see the dedication they have to their work.

In their own minds, they are the only ones who could possibly help their clients. In order to accomplish their tasks they will sacrifice their families, their money, their homes, their time, and their health on behalf of their clients. These ministers will be very pious about this. They may honestly feel that by sacrificing themselves for their clients, they are serving the Lord.

The problem with this syndrome is that it is not really unselfish. In a masochistic way these ministers gain a great deal of pleasure from their sacrifice. In fact, that pleasure is their motive, not the well-being of their clients. They are thinking more highly of themselves than they ought. They also want others, especially their clients, to appreciate their sacrifice. Instead of being other-centered, they are actually self-centered. These ministers are pharisaical in that they want to be known as the great ministers. They become jealous if their clients receive help from someone else.

The authority syndrome. It is easy for experienced ministers to feel that they have encountered every problem known to human beings. They are in danger of believing that they know what is right for everyone. They see themselves as final authorities and may violate their clients' rights to self-determination, attempting to make all their clients' decisions for them. They feel that they have the answer to everything their clients could possibly need; they consider it a waste of time to go through "this relationship-building stuff." These helpers are also on "ego trips." They have ceased to be the incarnation of God's love. They have become enamored by their own knowledge and skills. In so doing, they have ceased to function according to God's plan for social ministers.

Dysfunctional Persons

Dysfunctional persons experience obstacles to functioning in one or more domains of living which they cannot remove or cope with on their own.

Obstacles to Functioning

Something within persons is inadequate or prohibitive in removing or coping with the problem. Such persons do not have enough education, are not strong enough, may be handicapped in one way or another, or do not have the emotional strength or stability to cope. They are somehow inadequate for a specified task.

Environmental conditions are working against them. Not only must persons in need of help work with their problems, but they must also cope with their environment (home life) as well. Environment can breed illness, disease, and despair. It can afflict client systems relationally, physically, emotionally, and mentally. Environmental conditions often breed crime and delinquency and lead to apathy. As a result, clients appear to see no need to do anything about their situation. Poor environmental conditions can create despair over one's situation and bring about the loss of hope, destroying initiative.

Environmental conditions are not always solely to blame for every situation and condition. The individual's own personal choices are involved, even when the environmental condition is a contributing cause.

Inflexible rules, practices, or laws that do not allow for individual differences can be obstacles to functioning. Hiring policies can often contribute to the problem of a person needing work, as do hiring practices that discriminate against persons because of race, gender, or nationality. Rigid quotas stipulating that only a certain number of persons of a certain race or sex may be hired, regardless of the primary qualifications for the job, can be a problem. A parent who will not allow a child to make personal decisions can be an obstacle. In this situation the child will likely become rebellious. The practice of giving only certain kinds of jobs to black persons or Hispanics can create resentment or stifle initiative. The city or county street/road program that will not pave the streets in certain areas because only blacks, Mexicans, or poor whites live there is another example.

Accidents or disasters can cause sudden and extreme disability. Automobile accidents, fires, tornadoes, war, drought, floods, heart attacks, and cancer fit into this category.

The Role of Clients in Ministry Planning

Dysfunctional persons may not always recognize the need that others see in their situation. If they recognize a need, it may not be the one they are willing to deal with or to allow the minister to help them with. Ministers should recognize the right of persons to determine what their needs are and how they wish to deal with them.

> A young social minister visited the home of the Martin family. There were seven persons living in a two-room "shotgun" house. They had to take turns sleeping on the two beds and cot they had in the front room. Immediately the minister set about to find a larger house and more beds for the family. She found a seven-room house and additional beds and convinced the Martins to move into the house.

> Two weeks later she came back to visit and found the Martins living in two of the rooms and renting out the other five. They were not displeased with their new living arrangement; now they could get more money with which to do things like go to the movies, buy more toys, and have better food to eat. They did use the extra beds.

When social ministers attempt to work with persons in need they must *begin where persons are—how they perceive their problems and what they bring to the situation.* Persons cannot be helped until they are willing to be helped. They must be willing to tell someone else about their problems and allow that person to do things for them that they would ordinarily expect to do for themselves. They must allow the helper some control over their lives and their decisions, which is not an easy thing to do. Social ministers should be sensitive to this fact and do everything they can to guard each person's dignity and to rescue each person's pride.

> Many churches deliver Thanksgiving and/or Christmas baskets to the homes of needy families. Instead of taking food baskets to a person's home at Thanksgiving or Christmas, why do we not allow the parent to come by the church and pick up the baskets? Even if we provide

the transportation, it will be Dad or Mom who is bringing the food home to the family. This would guard their dignity and increase the children's pride in their father or mother.

When attempting to minister, why not allow persons in need to participate in decisions about what can be done? After all, the lives concerned are theirs. Ultimately, they will only make the adjustments that they choose to make. The task of social ministers is to enable clients to make those decisions by helping them to realize the options available and the ramifications of each options.

Ministry Programs

Social ministry programs are focused on Christ, person-centered, and need-oriented. They are focused on Christ in that they express love in the same way that he loved. They are motivated by His love and He is the model for our ministry. In the ministry reality is His, and when we are serving others we are serving Him. The New Testament contains both examples and admonitions for God's people engaging in this specific activity.

A person-centered ministry follows the model that Jesus left for us. Paul reminded us that even Christ did not minister to please Himself (Rom. 15:3). He did it for the person who needed His help at the moment and as a model for us to follow. Whatever we do in social ministry, we do because the person is in need. Our programs should be person-centered rather than program-centered. The program is to be the vehicle that delivers the service. The person in need is not there to serve the program. Our ministry is to be person-centered as opposed to people-centered. Program areas can relate to a population of people, but helping must ultimately be personal.

Our programs should be designed to alleviate an existing recognized need. We should not be developing programs just because someone else has one. The need may exist in their community in a way that it does not in ours. Ministry programs should reflect a recognized need and the resources with which to meet the need.

A suburban church began a day-care program. In one year they had enrolled over sixty children and reached over seventeen new families for the church, baptizing seven adults out of this group. Others heard about the excellent evangelistic results and got on the bandwagon. One church spent several thousand dollars remodeling their preschool area to meet the state regulations for child-care facilities. Teachers and other workers were hired. Supplies were purchased. Announcements were made. But on opening day only the children of the workers and one other child enrolled.

They had failed to develop the program around a recognized need in the community. The median age of persons living in that community was forty-three. There were very few small children in the area, and most of the working mothers with small children already had a satisfactory child-care arrangement. A simple survey would have revealed this to the church, if they had taken the time to do it.

This illustration highlights the importance of a person-centered and need-centered program plan. It also emphasizes another principle of social ministry programming: programs should have authentic Christlike motives. They should be designed to help because persons need help, not in order to do something else. Many programs have earned the distrust of the community because they are used as bait for adding members to the church. A cup of cold water should be given in the name of Christ because the person is thirsty, not because we want the person to feel obligated to listen to our evangelistic spiel.

Foreign missionaries learned years ago that it is easy to make "rice Christians." They found that when they gave out free rice at the end of the services, the buildings were full and every service produced many "converts." When the rice disappeared, so did the people. When the missionaries discovered this, they changed their policy. They continued to give rice to the people when it was available, but they distributed it at times other than the worship services. They continued to witness as they ministered, but they made it known that receiving the rice was not conditioned on one's church membership. They had fewer numbers to report, but they had more real converts.

Evangelism and Social Ministry

One of the key aspects of salvation is the conversion of persons to the lordship of Christ. This conversion is from the lordship of carnality and other authorities to a radical commitment to the dominion of Christ over all areas of life. By definition, Christian conversion has social and political implications. Delos Miles put it succinctly: "The plain truth is that whoever confesses, 'Jesus Christ is Lord,' is necessarily political to the extent that he or she has already delegitimated all other totalitarian claims of power. This is true today as it was in the first Christian century."[13] Social ministry draws its authority from the lordship of Christ. It also finds its basic model for integrating ministry and evangelism in how the early church interpreted that lordship.

Relating Social Ministry to Evangelism

Perhaps the most controversial question today is whether evangelism should be separated from the act of helping. Some feel that evangelism and social ministry are not compatible. One group feels that the social minister is in a position of power over the needy person; they consider it inappropriate to use this type of power to ask someone to make a profession of faith. This, it is argued, is what may lead to the "rice Christian" syndrome.

Others feel that when churches become involved in social ministries, they lose their evangelistic zeal. These churches, they argue, spend all of their energies putting "bandages" on the problems of the needy and never get down to the real need. The real need, they say, is the forgiveness of sin. Both arguments carry weight; sin is a real issue, and "baiting" persons is unethical.

Jesus sent out the seventy and told them to minister to the sick and others. They were also to bear witness to the kingdom of God (Luke 10:1-12). Obviously the biblical approach to ministry and evangelism is to integrate them. The motive for witnessing is that persons need a saving knowledge of and relationship with Jesus Christ. When we see persons in need of food, we should feed them because they need food. If in the course of our encounter we discover that they also need a saving relationship with Jesus Christ, we should witness to them. The act of concrete helping will in itself be a witness, and it will add credibility to our verbal witness.

In other words, our witness should be a matter of course. It is something we do naturally because we are Christians. Our helping with physical, emotional, mental, and relational needs should also be something we do as a matter of course because we are Christians.

---

[13]Delos Miles, *Evangelism and Social Involvement* (Nashville: Broadman Press, 1986), 40.

As we do either, we must be conscious of needs for the other type of help. Our programming should reflect this attitude. Our planning should include helping because there is a need and witnessing because there is a need.

> A social minister at a mission center in Fort Worth, Texas, was interviewing a homeless person. When asked if he was a Christian, the homeless person answered, "Yes. I am a Baptist. Two years ago I was saved by a Father. I don't remember his name, but he was a priest in a Baptist church in San Antonio. I've been going to Baptist churches all of my life. My parents had me baptized when I was a baby, in a Baptist church in Del Rio."

> The poor man was obviously lying. However, he was obviously fearful that he would not get any food or clothing if he did not tell the minister what the minister wanted to hear. The social minister helped the man with the clothing and food he needed and then shared his own testimony about how he came to know Christ in a life-transforming way. Although the man did not make a profession of faith, he did hear the message and experienced a bit of God's grace as well.

Experiences such as this have led many social ministers to avoid even talking with persons about Christ or attempting to lead them to Christ. They seem to be content to leave evangelism to pastors, Sunday School teachers, and others. They may not be anti-evangelistic, but they have doubts about the conversion of the needy persons they encounter.

The minister should be sensitive to the spiritual readiness of the one asking for help and begin by attempting to provide what the person asks for. Then the minister should look for an appropriate opportunity to share a testimony or a positive witness for Christ in such a way that the person does not feel undue pressure to respond. Remember, Jesus never forced Himself on anyone. The key here is *intentionality*. Witnessing is not left to chance. The "cup of cold water" is given in the name of Christ.

Further investigation of declining churches and denominations that stress social ministry or social action may reveal that they dropped evangelism from their list of priorities, replacing it with social action. Had they continued to stress evangelism along with their emphasis on social action, their stories might have been different. Indeed, there are some outstanding examples in which this has been the case.

Styles of Evangelism

A variety of behaviors may be termed *evangelism*. Some define evangelism as the intentional act of helping persons find peace with God. Others think of evangelism as proclaiming the good news of Jesus Christ to individuals and groups, encouraging them to accept Him as their Lord and Savior. This would include both individual soul-winning and mass evangelistic efforts. Still others see evangelism as all that a Christian does in the name of Christ: social ministry, education, life-style, Bible teaching, and preaching, as well as personal soul-winning and revival preaching.

Confrontational evangelism uses an aggressive approach by personal soul-winners who challenge others to pray the prayer of repentance and accept Christ as Lord and Savior. Programs such as Evangelism Explosion, Continuing Witness Training, Campus Crusade, and others have been very effective in leading persons to make professions of faith, using this approach.

Life-style evangelism is less direct and calls for the evangelist to demonstrate his/her relationship with Christ in day-to-day activities. A life-style evangelist seeks to make people aware of Christ through the type of life he or she lives and to encourage persons to ask about the source of his or her spirituality. Thus, opportunities for personal soul-winning appear, and the evangelist is prepared to share the good news with the inquirer.[14]

Demonstration evangelism calls for the evangelist to emulate Christ and His concern for the physical, social, and emotional needs of persons, along with the spiritual. The evangelist demonstrates God's love for persons who are in need of food, drink, shelter, medical care, and acceptance by meeting their needs. Along with this action, the evangelist tells those who receive the help about the One who cares about them both temporally and eternally. This approach calls for a high level of sensitivity to the needs of persons. It relies on the leading of the Holy Spirit and depends on Him to convict and guide in the evangelistic effort.

A key word in any effective form of evangelism is *intentionality*. The New Testament leaves no doubt that all Christians are to *be* His witnesses with every deed and in every place they serve. Com-

---

[14]W. Oscar Thompson, *Concentric Circles of Concern* (Nashville: Broadman Press, 1981), 1-27.

mands made in the Great Commission and in Acts 1:8 are impera-tive. They are not debatable or negotiable. Whatever the task, it has implications for evangelism. As long as the Christian has life, every moment is to be used for an intentional witness for Christ.

Evangelism as a Helping Function

Evangelism has served to broaden the scope of ministry. It led the earliest Christians to minister to every person without regard to gender, race, nationality, socioeconomic status, caste, or physical condition. This form of evangelism caused Christianity to spread rapidly to all of the known world. It also formed a bond that sustained Christians through some of the most severe persecutions in their history. It enabled the early church to break down enor-mous walls of resistance and turn those who were their persecutors into their converts.

Today's evangelism recognizes the need for the transforming power of God in the lives of all persons. This is true of homeless persons as well as those who live in high-rise apartments. Unsaved persons exist in a hostile environment that they do not understand or like. Whether persons are Christian or not, God is their primary environment (Ps. 139). Those who are not in harmony with God are out of harmony with their environment. The trees, the sky, the land-scape, the sun, and the thunder and lightning are God's creations and they testify of Him. Every person who is not in right relation-ship with the Creator is incomplete and uncomfortable. It is futile to attempt to transform persons' living arrangements, provide food and clothing, and assuage their anxieties and depressions without helping them to find peace with God.[15]

Summary and Conclusions

A philosophy of social ministry includes the belief that min-istry is a primary function of the church. It is an integral part of every aspect of church life. This inclusive philosophy has applica-tion for individual Christians, individual congregations, associa-tions of congregations, and denominations. Christian social ministers recognize the worth, dignity, and integrity of all persons, regardless of age, gender, race, ethnicity, national origin, or reli-gious beliefs. Social ministers draw this attitude from their knowl-

---

[15]Jay Adams, *A Theology of Christian Counseling* (Grand Rapids: Zondervan Pub-lishing Company, 1986), 34-40.

edge and understanding of the ministry of Christ. They seek to integrate biblical principles, prayer, and evangelism with their skills of helping dysfunctional persons. Growing out of this philosophy is a commitment to planning and implementing ministry programs that are Spirit-directed and empowered, person-centered, and need-oriented.

Exercises for Review and Examination

1. Define the term *social ministry.*

2. Relate the social ministry function to the other major functions of the church.

3. List and discuss each of the seven principles of social ministry.

4. Discuss the qualities, attitudes, and dangers involved in being an effective social minister.

5. Briefly discuss four major obstacles to functioning that may result in a need for help.

6. Write a four-page paper on your philosophy of social ministry.

Chapter Six

Methods and Skills for Social Ministry

Goal: A study of this chapter should enable the social minister to gain knowledge of the various methods, skills, and tools used in the practice of social ministry.

Objectives: The minister . . .

1. defines the terms *methods* and *skills*.
2. describes the use of such methods as casework, marital intervention, family intervention, group intervention, community intervention, and organizational intervention.
3. discusses skills such as information gathering, problem assessment, strategy planning, implementation, and evaluation of interventions.
4. explains how knowledge of human behavior and the exercise of prayer, Bible study, and faith serve as tools for social ministry.

This chapter is divided into two major segments. The first segment deals with methods for practice; the second describe specific skills used in the practice of social ministry. Methods refer to such functions as casework, case management, individual counseling, marital counseling, family counseling, group counseling, educational and support group work, community intervention, community planning, and social action. Skills refer to specific actions used in each method such as interviewing, teaching, planning, resource acquisition, linking/referring, advocacy, confrontation, and conflict resolution.

Methods in Social Ministry

Intervention with Individuals

As we have seen in previous chapters, the ultimate focus of social ministry is individuals. These individuals may be helped in one-to-one relationships, in groups, in organizations, and in the community. This method usually means that the approach is one-to-one, such as individual counseling, casework, or case management. This process is called *social casework*. Casework is most often used in social service agencies. It is the oldest method in social work.[1] A person who needs material resources receives these individually. When the needs are emotional or mental, the person is helped through one-to-one counseling. This form of help is limited concerning relational problems, but a skillful helper can provide advice and guidance.

> Opel came to the church office one day in late winter. She wanted to talk with someone who could help her with a problem. She would not share the nature of this problem with the receptionist. Janet, the church's Director of Outreach and Community Ministries, overheard her and asked if she could help. The receptionist had tried to make an appointment with the pastor for her, but she was resisting. Janet asked her to come into her office where they could talk. Opel was relieved that there was a woman at the church who seemed competent and would take time to listen.
>
> She was having a problem with her husband. Their relationship was deteriorating rapidly. Her husband couldn't understand her "female" problems. She had been reared with the idea that good women just do not talk about such things with men. Janet suggested that they set regular times for her to come and talk and advised her to make an appointment to see a doctor. Opel did not have a family physician she could turn to, and she feared that

---

[1] Robert W. Roberts and Robert H. Nee, *Theories of Social Casework* (Chicago: University of Chicago Press, 1970).

115

having to pay a doctor would make her husband even more angry with her.

Janet obtained her permission to set up an appointment at the Outpatient Diagnostic Clinic operated at the church by volunteer doctors and nurses. She would not be required to pay if she could not. The doctor was able to prescribe medication that eased the physical problem and he gave her some advice and a booklet she could share with her husband. For a few weeks she continued to come to visit with Janet. She and her husband eventually began to attend Sunday School, where they made new friends and became part of a fellowship group.

This case illustrates an important fact in casework practice: human needs are multifaceted; therefore, the social minister must be prepared to help the individual with more than one problem. Opel was experiencing personal anxiety related to her physical problem, her relationship with her husband, and their financial limitations. She did not have an available social support system from which to draw emotional support. We can guess that her husband was also experiencing a great deal of stress about their situation. Therefore, he was unable to provide the support Opel needed at home. The various factors of Opel's problem interacted with each other in a negative manner. The social minister's task was to choose one facet of the problem with which to intervene directly, and to help Opel find ways of managing the stress of the others.

This situation took place in a church where the pastor was not threatened by his staff. He was not afraid to allow another staff person to utilize her competence in counseling. The social minister must be sensitive to the mind-set of the pastor in such cases, since the pastor is the staff leader.

Intervention with Couples

This method uses the skills of marital intervention.[2] Couples with relationship problems in such areas as communication, sexual adjustment, family planning, and role performance may need the services of a professional social minister.

---

[2]For an in-depth study of marital intervention read such books as Peter A. Martin, *A Marital Therapy Manual* (New York: Brunner/Mazel, Publishers, 1976); Edwin J. Thomas, *Marital Communication and Decision Making* (New York: Free Press, 1977); R. Taylor Segraves, *Marital Therapy* (New York: Plenum Medical Book Company, 1982).

Dean and Audrey had grown up in the church. After their marriage they continued to attend worship services, but they did not join the couples Sunday School class. After a few months their attendance at worship services became more sporadic, and eventually they completely stopped attending. Mike, the Church and Community Minister, went to visit them. He could hear a loud argument through the closed door before he knocked.

Dean came to the door. When he recognized Mike, he put on a smile and invited him to come in. Audrey was not in the room at the time; she had gone to the bedroom. When she came out, Mike noticed that her eyes were swollen as though she had been crying. She made an attempt to show that nothing was wrong.

Mike decided to take a direct approach. He confronted them gently with what he had heard and suggested that help was available for them if they wanted it. Audrey began to cry openly, and Dean went to her and put his arms around her. Dean looked as though he might cry also.

They told Mike that they had been having some difficulty in their relationship. They did not feel that they could talk with anyone at the church because they did not think church families would understand. They were thinking of divorce, although they declared that they loved each other. Mike assured them that others had experienced similar difficulties and that there was help available at the church. He made an appointment for them to begin couple therapy and encouraged them to attend a couples communication workshop sponsored by the Young Adult Department.

After six weeks of therapy and attending the workshop, Dean and Audrey have become regulars in the Young Adult Department, and both are now singing in the choir. Dean has begun playing on the church's basketball team. They show signs of growing in Christ and in love with each other.

Intervening with couples calls for the social minister to be aware that the work to be done is not with the individuals involved. The interventions target the relationship between those individuals. The case of Audrey and Dean illustrates this point. Dean and Audrey were experiencing an acute dysfunction in their relationship. They cared about each other, but the conflict between them was leading to the dissolution of the marriage. They did not think that church people would understand, so they felt unable to call upon Christian friends for emotional and spiritual support.

By using couple therapy in the intervention, the social minister was able to help them deal with the relationship conflicts that were separating them. Encouraging them to attend the couples communication workshop enabled them to develop better communication skills so that they could grow in their relationship. By encouraging them to attend the Sunday School class, the minister helped them to develop a social and spiritual support system that could sustain them in the future.

Intervention with Families

Family intervention focuses on the needs of whole families. Built upon the family systems theory, family intervention recognizes that when one aspect of a family's life is out of balance, the whole family is at risk. Intervention with a family requires that the worker focus on the relationships of family members and how effective they are in performing their prescribed roles. This includes the relationships among family members and how each family member's relationships with other systems outside the family interface. Those relationships outside the family include such systems as work, school, church, recreation, friends, and relatives.[3]

> The Craig family had lived in the neighborhood near the church for almost three years. The children had attended Vacation Bible School, and occasionally the family would attend a special function at the church. The oldest child, ten-year-old Vacua, had begun to attend Sunday School.

> One day Mrs. Craig called the church to see if anybody there might help them. The son, Billy, had been caught shoplifting at the local mall. The parents were devastated. There had never been a member of their family on either side involved with the law. They couldn't understand

---

[3]For an in-depth study of family therapy read such books as: Betty Carter and Monica McGoldrick, eds., *The Changing Family Life Cycle* (New York: Gardner Press, 1988); Lynn Hoffman, *Foundations of Family Therapy* (New York: Basic Books, 1981); and Curtis Janzen and Oliver Harris, *Family Treatment in Social Work Practice* (Itasca, Ill.: F. E. Peacock Publishers, 1986).

what had gone wrong. Why would Billy do such a thing? They were good people, she declared.

The Community Minister, Kathy, had earned an M.A. degree in church social services at the seminary and an M.S.S.W. at the university. She was a licensed marriage and family therapist. The pastor, who had received the call, suggested that Mrs. Craig speak with the Community Minister. Mrs. Craig called, and Kathy suggested that she would come to the Craigs' home to visit with the whole family. She stressed that it would be important for the whole family to be present. Fees for family counseling would be assessed on a sliding scale, based upon the family's ability to pay.

Kathy made the visit and observed the interaction among the family members. She discovered that the children had many toys. However, there seemed to be little affection shown among family members. Their primary emotional interaction seemed to be expressions of hostility.

Mr. and Mrs. Craig did not sit near each other. The family's communication seemed to center around Mrs. Craig. Mr. Craig said very little and seemed somewhat annoyed that Mrs. Craig had invited Kathy to their home. He stated that their family could handle their own problems. Mrs. Craig said that they had not been doing a very good job of it recently, and she felt that they needed someone to help them sort things out.

Kathy made an appointment to visit with them on a weekly basis. She discovered that Billy had been in constant trouble at school. These episodes of Billy's seemed to coincide with bouts of severe disagreements between Mr. and Mrs. Craig. The Craigs agreed to work on their relationship with each other and to find ways of showing affection and support for every member of the family. After two months of regular sessions, Billy was no longer getting into trouble, and the family agreed with Kathy that therapy was no longer necessary.

Although they did not resume attending Kathy's church, they did begin to attend their own church on a regular basis. They have since referred several families to the church for help.

Some social ministers prefer to conduct family therapy sessions in their offices. They feel that they are at a disadvantage when they are "on the family's turf." There are, however, several advantages to intervening with families in their own homes. (1) The minister can learn more about families by observing them in their primary environments. (2) Families will be more relaxed in the familiar environments of their own homes. (3) Families may actually follow through with decisions they make in their own homes as opposed to decisions made in the unfamiliar environment of a therapist's office. The solutions more naturally become theirs.

Another form of family intervention is family life education. This includes such programs as parenting and guidance classes, family communication workshops, family enrichment weekends, new family workshops for expectant fathers and mothers, and family financial management classes. Other family intervention includes such programs as family housing option counseling for older persons and their families, retirement counseling, and counseling with adult children of older parents. In addition, family interventions may include direct services to families in need of material services such as emergency family food distribution, family clothing distribution, assistance with family housing, and assistance with employment.

Intervention with Groups

When two or more people have a single purpose, quality, or problem in common, they are a group. The church is full of groups. The primary group in the church is the family. The staff is a group. Sunday School and Discipleship Training use group methods almost exclusively. There are men's groups, women's groups, youth groups, adult groups, single adult groups, senior adult groups, and children's groups. In the neighborhood there are racial groups, political groups, age groups, recreation groups, civic groups, and educational groups. The church congregation is a group.

The social minister who is conscious of group work principles and has a knowledge of group dynamics can accomplish a great deal with these groups, both inside the church and outside in the community.[4]

---

[4]For an in-depth study of group-work, study: Lawrence Shulman, *The Skills of Helping Individuals and Groups* (Itasca, Ill.: F. E. Peacock Publishers, 1991).

Most of the problems persons experience have group implications. Any trauma that affects one member of the family has an effect on all the rest of the family. In the same manner, anything that happens in a church group will affect the whole church. This is true both in a positive and a negative sense.

Sam, a minister with adults in an inner-city church, noticed that there was a large number of names on the Young Adult Sunday School roll of persons who had not attended in over a year. He decided to call some of these persons and see what was happening. He discovered that many of them were divorced and did not feel comfortable in the regular department, which was made up mostly of couples. They did not wish to go back to the College Department either. So they simply quit attending. At first they continued to attend the worship services, but finally that too dropped out of their schedules.

Sam asked several of them if they would attend a class for persons who were divorced or widowed. Many felt that would be awkward if it was at the regular time. Feeling that he was not getting anywhere, he decided to ask them for suggestions. He invited two men and three women to meet him at the local coffee shop on Sunday morning at 8:00. They decided meeting at the coffee shop each Sunday morning would be a good idea. They would have Bible study and a sharing time.

Sam divided the names and telephone numbers among the five, and each invited a number of persons to join them the next Sunday from 8:00 to 9:15. More than twenty persons showed up for this session. The coffee shop allowed them to use the banquet room and order from the menu. Divorced persons from other churches joined them, and in a year there were three such groups with a total of seventy-three enrolled. (They were counted in the regular Sunday School attendance.) Many personal needs were met through these groups. Bible study, prayer, and sharing was the program, and this combination helped each person to grow personally and spiritually. Two of the groups asked to have a department of their own at the church during the regular Sunday School hour. The other one is still meeting at the coffee shop.

Groups can function as sharing groups, recreation groups, educational groups, prayer groups, Bible study groups, and therapy groups, to name a few. The alert minister can use these to help persons experiencing various levels of dysfunction.

Intervention with Organizations

Organizations such as the Public Health Department, the City Planning Commission, the Police Public Relations Department, the YMCA or YWCA, Adult Basic Education, and senior citizens' agencies offer excellent opportunities for the church to expand its witness. Often these agencies and others such as the Salvation Army, the Mental Health Association, and Family Service Association can be invited to provide expert service to persons with whom the church is ministering. Often they will reciprocate by calling the church when some person in the church's neighborhood needs help. They usually have well-trained professionals who are very willing to aid the church in training volunteers.

Sometimes the church ministers directly to the organizations by providing a needed service to them.

A minister in a rural church discovered that no single office existed in the county where a person could find the names, addresses, and telephone numbers of the available social services in the county and the surrounding area. The telephone book provided a start, but it did not have the services listed in one place. He approached the county attorney's office with the idea of trying to locate all these services and listing them in one resource book so that each could know what the others were doing and where to call for specific services.

The county attorney agreed to have his secretary call every person or agency they could locate in the region and invite them to meet at the courthouse. The number became too large for the office to hold them, so they moved to the fellowship hall at the church, which was one block off the square. Persons had been asked if they knew of other services in the region and if they would call them and invite them to the meeting. Thus they came up with a relatively complete listing.

The church volunteered to photocopy the material, and the attorney agreed to have his secretary type the originals. The group voted to let the church handle the distribution of the resource books. Each agency with a listing made a contribution to help defray the expenses of reproducing the books and mailing them.

The church soon became the center of activity for persons needing social services. A volunteer staff was enlisted and trained to operate an information and referral program, which coordinated all the social services for the area.

Intervention with Communities

In addition to working with organizations, the church can serve as a positive force for needed change in the community.[5] This can be done by getting the people of a neighborhood together to discuss and plan strategies for changing some problematic situation in the area.

One church, located in a poverty area of the city, invited all the citizens of the area to use the fellowship hall for a meeting to discuss street lighting in the neighborhood. Mugging and thefts were common. People did not dare get out on the street at night alone because of the growing crime rate in the area. The minister of the church was elected to be the chairperson of the group, and a delegation was sent to the next city council meeting. There they presented their request for more streetlights and more police protection.

The council heard them politely, but nothing was done. Two months later the community group met again. At the suggestion of the minister, every person who was registered to vote went to the council chambers the next time the council met. They filled the room and presented their case to the council again, reminding them that this was an election year. They were heard. Within a month the streetlights were installed, and police patrols were more frequent in the area. The crime rate was reduced by over 50 percent. As a result, that church has a much more effective witness in the community.

Churches have led in organizing such programs as community betterment organizations, neighborhood cleanup activities,

---

[5]For a more in-depth study of community intervention, study Thomas M. Meenaghan, Robert O. Washington, and Robert M. Ryan, *Macro Practice in the Human Services* (New York: Free Press, 1982).

neighborhood youth centers, community safety patrols, and Crime Watch programs. When there is a need in the community, the alert church can provide leadership and resources that may enable the community to do something about the situation. In so doing, Christ is honored, the weak and powerless receive justice, and God's will is done.

One danger must be noted. Some churches that have become involved in social service and/or action programs of this type have lost their evangelistic zeal. This occurrence creates a spiritually anemic church that becomes just another social service agency. It does not have to happen.[6]

Skills for Social Ministry

The methods listed earlier have certain basic or generic skills in common. Let's discuss these skills and provide a framework for using them in the practice of social ministry.

Information Gathering

The skill of gathering information comes first not only because of chronology, but also because it is very important in the helping process. The minister must gather as much information as possible before entering into a helping situation. Continuing to gather information while the relationship is in process is also important. God knows what is in the minds and hearts of persons. He has given us the senses and the abilities to gather data and assess it so that we, too, can know what we need to know in order to help persons.

Before determining a strategy of intervention, information should be gathered regarding the cause(s) of the dysfunction of the client system. Teare and McPheeters suggest four categories of obstacles to client system functioning: personal limitations; environmental deficiencies; rigid laws, rules, policies, or regulations; and/or catastrophes.[7] It would be helpful for social ministers to use this conceptual model as a guide for gathering information. The figure following is part of a larger conceptual model developed for social ministers, to be used in the assessment of people's problems.

---

[6]Lyle E. Schaller, *Community Organization* (Nashville: Abingdon Press, 1966).
[7]Robert J. Teare and Harold L. McPheeters, *Manpower Utilization in Social Welfare* (Atlanta: Southern Regional Education Board, 1970), 11-17.

CAUSE OF DYSFUNCTION			
Personal Limitations	Environmental Deficiencies	Rigid Laws, Policies, Regulations, Practices	Catastrophes
(I)	(II)	(III)	(IV)

The following are facets of the information-gathering process.

Observing. Observation will tell you a great deal about a person through: appearance, behavior, expressions, attitudes, mannerisms, dress, personal grooming, and eye contact.[8] According to Bloom, the worker should observe three rules when gathering information through observation. First, while looking at the momentary scene, make a mental comparison between it and some larger pattern of events. How does it fit into ordinary, everyday events? Second, reduce the number of possible concepts of which that event may be an instance. Is this a pattern, or is it a one-time happening? Third, test your interpretation against other information you may have about the client's social history.[9] Social ministers can learn a great deal about persons by visiting in the home. Noting the condition of items such as the yard, automobile, house, floor, furniture, sidewalk, driveway, walls, curtains, and lighting can provide useful information about the client.

> Janet, a Minister of Outreach and Community Ministries at Calvary Baptist Church, received a call from Susan, requesting financial help to pay the utility bills. She also wanted some food, if possible, because they were having trouble with the local grocery store. Their bank account had been "messed up," and several checks had "bounced." Janet suggested that she would visit Susan in her home since she was going to be in that area in a few minutes anyway.

---

[8]Gerard Nierenberg and Henry Calero, *How to Read a Person Like a Book* (New York: Pocket Books, 1971), 7-172.

[9]Martin Bloom, *Introduction to the Drama of Social Work* (Itasca, Ill.: F. E. Peacock Publishers, 1990), 441.

When she arrived she noticed beer cans strewn over the lawn and front porch. A child with a dirty face and equally dirty diapers (they looked as if they had not been changed since the night before) was standing behind a screened door. The screen was torn and hanging loose at one corner. Inside, the floor was covered with clutter, and the worn-out carpet had several hard greasy spots. The stench that greeted Janet was almost unbearable, but she managed to sit in a straight-backed chair while Susan sat on the new divan. There was a new color console television in the room. Susan immediately said that they were renting it at "only" eighteen dollars per week.

From where she sat, Janet could see a stack of unwashed pots and pans in the sink. Roaches were climbing up the walls, and a large one ran across her foot while she was talking with Susan. Needless to say, it was difficult for Janet to keep her mind on what Susan was trying to tell her about her family situation.

When Janet compiles her information, she will have many observational perceptions to include in addition to what Susan shared with her. The social minister's observations will enhance her ability to assess the needs of the client. She will make note of such things as attitude, pride, personal habits, and financial irresponsibility. She will determine if there are matters in the environment that are working against the client. She will also attempt to see if there are resources available within the client system and/or the environment that may be tapped for the client's benefit.

Taking a "windshield survey" can also provide useful observations for program development. Social ministers who drive through the streets of a neighborhood at varying times of the day can learn a great deal about the constituency of the local church area. The way the lawns, houses, driveways, and sidewalks are kept will speak of the pride persons take in their environment. If there are many children playing in the yards and on the sidewalks, social ministers may assume that there are a large number of younger families in the area. In some neighborhoods there will be bicycles for older children, tricycles for younger ones. Toys may be seen on walkways and in driveways.

If there is an unusual number of older cars with wide rear tires, there will likely be a number of older adolescents in the area. If the lawns are full of older vehicles in various states of disrepair and the houses are not well kept, this community is likely populated by a lower socioeconomic group. If the houses are older but well kept, and few toys, bicycles and tricycles are visible, older persons probably populate this neighborhood.

Interviewing. The most effective information-gathering technique is interviewing. This is the process where clients tell the social minister the things they wish the minister to know. Interviewing involves observation, questioning, and listening. It has three functions: (1) information or social study; (2) problem assessment and decision making; and (3) therapy. Interviewing is involved in all phases of the helping process from intake to termination.[10]

Questioning is the basic tool of the interview. First the client must be heard and observed, and then the social minister should ask specific questions for clarification. In order to obtain a useful social history, he or she must cover certain areas: physical health, income, employment, family, housing, education, leisure, community, personal feelings, hostilities, disappointments, and religious beliefs. These are called the "domains of living."[11]

In addition to discovering the basic social history, the minister needs to know what difficulties exist and the reasons for them. Many churches and centers use an intake form for the basic information they need and then gather additional information in the interview. Sometimes the minister will need to fill out the form for the client during the intake interview. This usually happens when the client is not literate or when he is emotionally unable to cope with written questions.

Listening is also a basic tool of interviewing. Listening is more than keeping one's mouth closed while the other person is talking;[12] it is trying to hear what the other person is actually saying. Ministers must hear the requests in the form they are brought to them. This is called the "presenting problem," and it is often not the most important or "real problem." It is, though, the only one that the client wishes to talk about at the present moment. Therefore, ministers must listen carefully and actively, encouraging clients to tell everything they can about their situation.[13] If clients feel

---

[10]For more in-depth discussions of the skills of interviewing see Louise C. Johnson, *Social Work Practice* (Boston: Allyn and Bacon, 1989), 186-195; Charles Zastrow, *The Practice of Social Work* (Chicago: Dorsey Press, 1989), 56-67.

[11]Teare and McPheeters, *Manpower Utilization in Social Welfare*, 13.

[12]Lyman Steil, Larry Barker, and Kittie Watson, *Effective Listening* (Reading, Mass.: Addison-Wesley Publishing Co., 1983), 11.

[13]Robert Bolton, *People Skills* (New York: Simon and Schuster, 1979), 27-114.

that ministers have listened to their stories, they may be more inclined to share more important problems. The intensity with which ministers listen will be a clue to clients regarding the authenticity of concern.

While listening to the presenting problem ministers should also listen to what is not being said—what clients are leaving out, what clients are avoiding, what the tone of voice is saying. Clients will usually test the environment to see whether the minister is easy or hard to deal with. They want to get what they are asking for, and they will often play whatever role they think ministers want them to play in order to get it.

Surveying. Surveying, in addition to observing, can be done in three ways: door-to-door interviews, printed surveys, and agency interviews. The door-to-door type of interview should employ an instrument (a questionnaire that is concise and can be answered quickly and easily). No questions should be included that cannot be easily answered by the householder. Generally, questions should not be asked of individual householders if the information can be obtained from printed materials or from other agencies.

Most surveyors choose to use a random-sample approach rather than door-to-door interviewing. For example, if surveyors need to know the general attitude of the neighborhood regarding the most pressing needs, they might choose to interview persons living in every third house on each block. They feel that this will provide sufficient information and will also be more efficient than a door-to-door approach.

On the other hand, if more specific information about each family in the neighborhood is desirable, every family must be questioned. Alpha Melton, founder of the Baptist Good Will Center and the Social Work Department at Southwestern Seminary in Fort Worth, Texas, began a day-care program at the Center in the mid-1950s. She had observed a need but felt that she must get more information, so she went to each family in the community and asked if they would use the Center if one were instituted. When she opened the Center, several families were already committed to using it. Hundreds have been blessed through that program over the more than forty years of the Center's existence.

Another approach involves mailing a printed questionnaire to either a random sample of a population or to every address in a community. These questionnaires should be designed so that the respondents will be able to complete them with relative ease. For example, if it is important that respondents make a choice of printed responses rather than write a response, this should be clearly explained and illustrated (if possible). Nothing should be assumed about the respondents' ability to understand how to fill out the questionnaire.

Telephoning can also be an efficient and effective method for this type of information gathering. A "crisscross" reference telephone book, which has telephone numbers listed by street rather than by the alphabet, is helpful.

Printed material can be scanned to discover what others have already discovered about the neighborhood. Census reports, city Planning Commission studies, school district studies, and Chamber of Commerce studies are examples. Many of these can be viewed at the agencies' offices. Some of the reports are available at the public library.

Agency interviews can provide excellent information about the community. Agency workers must keep up-to-date information on hand at all times. They have done the studies just mentioned, and they have other useful information available to the social minister.

Surveying is an excellent way to discover gaps in services that might be filled by a church social ministry program. A *gap in service* is evident when certain needs have been identified in the community but no private, public, or church agency has instituted a program to meet those needs.

Researching. Research refers to the process of forming a hypothesis, gathering information (data), testing the hypothesis, evaluating the results, and postulating a thesis. In other words, the minister has an idea regarding a technique or program that might serve as a solution to a social problem. Resources are gathered and the program is implemented. The program is evaluated, results are noted and conclusions are formulated. If it worked, how? If it did not function as expected, why? Will the same approach be used again, or should something different be attempted next? Why? Answers to these questions can aid social ministers with the assessment and future intervention strategy planning.

Problem Assessment

This process is often called *diagnosis*. The function of assessment is to clarify the problem and to determine what should be done about it. It is based upon an assumption that adequate information has been gathered on all areas of the client's life (domains of living), and each area of life can be evaluated to determine the client's level of functioning in each. If everything seems to be going as it should in an area, the client is in a state of "high-level wellness." If some minor difficulty is occurring in an area, he is in a state of "well-being." If something needs to be done to prevent a worse situation, he is at the "mildly dysfunctional" state. If matters are getting critical and it seems that complete collapse in an area is imminent, the client is in a state of "acute dysfunction." If collapse has already occurred, he is in a state of "chronic dysfunction." The first step is to determine how well the person, couple, family, group, organization, or community is functioning.

David L. Levine and Derrel R. Watkins have developed a matrix for use in gathering information, assessing the level of client functioning and developing a strategy of intervention. The first part of the matrix calls for the minister to determine the client system's level of functioning as illustrated in the following figure.

STATUS OF FUNCTIONING				
High-level Wellness	Well-being	Mild or Early Dysfunction	Acute Dysfunction	Chronic Dysfunction
Well-being	Stress	Problem	Crisis	Dysfunction
(I)	(II)	(III)	(IV)	(V)

The original Levine matrix called for five levels of functioning: (I) high-level wellness—a condition requiring no intervention; (II) well-being—a condition that might lead to an intervention designed to protect the client system from deterioration; (III) mild or early dysfunction—a condition requiring prompt and specific intervention in order to prevent further deterioration; (IV) acute dysfunction—a condition requiring extensive and immediate intervention; (V) chronic dysfunction—a condition requiring social rehabilitation. Teare and McPheeters, using the Levine matrix as a model, changed the designations of each level of functioning to well-being; stress; problem; crisis; and dysfunction.[14]

---

[14]Teare and McPheeters, *Manpower Utilization in Social Welfare*, 15.

As the social minister interviews the client all areas of the client's life should be considered, both separately and as a whole—separately, so that determination can be made as to where the client is hurting the most, what is causing the dysfunction, and what can be done about it; as a whole, because any change in one area of life will affect all the other areas. A decision about what needs to be done should take into account which intervention will most likely effect the most positive change in this client's life.

Some feel that all of these may be dealt with by persons making professions of faith in Christ, praying, and becoming members of local congregations of Christians. This will certainly help with some needs; however, God has provided us with knowledge that may be used in developing a comprehensive helping ministry. When the social minister intervenes with a client system, it is essential that both the minister and the client understand what is hindering the client.

At this juncture, clients must participate in decision making concerning their needs. Ultimately, it is their lives that are at stake. Decisions must be generated for the benefit of the client, or the whole helping effort will be ineffective.[15]

Marcia went away to college after graduating from high school. She later dropped out to begin living with Jimmy. Jimmy came from a broken family and did not want to "get all entangled in marriage." He convinced Marcia that they would be happier if they just lived together and enjoyed each other without the strings that matrimony "tied people up with." Marcia's parents had reared her in the church, and they were very disturbed by her decision.

After two months of sharing an apartment, Marcia became pregnant. Jimmy was upset and insisted that she have an abortion. She refused and came home to live with her parents. They took her to the church counseling center, where a trained social worker/counselor worked with her.

The counselor allowed her to talk without interruption for over forty-five minutes. She spoke of bitterness toward Jimmy and her parents and the church. She expressed hostility toward her father and mother because

---

[15]James K. Whittaker and Elizabeth M. Tracy, *Social Treatment* (New York: Aldine De Gruyter, 1989), 73–86.

of their "rigid, old-fashioned morals." She felt that if they had been more easy-going while she was growing up, she would have learned to cope with sex as other girls did and not feel so guilty now. Marcia did not have a job since her education was incomplete. The doctor had warned her that she could have difficulties in carrying the child. She sometimes felt like killing herself, and that made her feel even more guilty. She did not dare go around her friends anymore because she was getting "big." She never got out of the house except to go to the doctor or to the counseling center, which she was not sure would do her any good anyway.

While Marcia's perceptions about the causes of her problems were not accurate, they were the ones the social minister had to deal with before any other solutions could be found. Using the conceptual model that follows, the social minister was able to determine that Marcia's level of functioning was IV-1 (Acutely Dysfunctional). The primary cause of her problems were (I) Personal Limitations and (II) Environmental Deficiencies. Her own decisions and her pregnancy were at the root of her problem. The college environment, her family, and the community situation were also considered as contributing factors.

Intervention Strategy Planning

After assessing the problem and determining the level of functioning and the cause(s) of the dysfunction, the social minister can develop a strategy of intervention. There are five strategy categories. (A) *Needs providing*—this is the least involved strategy. It calls for the worker to provide basic material or information to the client system, such as food, clothing, lodging, or transportation; (B) *Problem solving*—this level of intervention calls for a didactic (educational) function on the part of the worker who teaches problem-solving skills or provides training and instructions that the client systems can use in resolving their own problems; (C) *Conflict resolving*—this is the most sophisticated level of intervention because it calls for counseling and psychotherapy to resolve dysfunctional interpersonal and/or intrapersonal conflicts; (D) *System change*—this is called for when something in the client's environment creates an obstacle to functioning, such as rigid laws, rules, regulations, or practices. System change also deals with advocating for the client system with other systems who might be in position to help but who, for whatever reason, are not helping; (E) *No intervention*—this

Assessment in Christian Social Ministries

STATUS OF FUNCTIONING				
High-level Wellness	Well-being	Mild or Early Dysfunction	Acute Dysfunction	Chronic Dysfunction
Well-being	Stress	Problem	Crisis	Dysfunction
I	II	III	IV	V
1 / 2 / 3	1 / 2 /3	1 / 2 / 3	1 / 2 / 3	1 / 2 / 3
CAUSE OF DYSFUNCTION				
Personal Limitations	Environmental Deficiencies		Policies, Laws, Rigid Rules, Regulations	Catastrophes
(I)	(II)		(III)	(IV)
STRATEGY OF INTERVENTION				
Needs Providing	Problem Solving	Conflict Resolving	System Change	No Intervention
A	B	C	D	E

may be the choice of either the worker or the client system, when to take specific action could cause more harm. It would also be chosen when it is important that the client systems work on resolving their own problems rather than becoming dependent upon the church for meeting all their needs.

Once the decision is made to do something about the problem, social ministers should then work with the client systems to determine how to proceed. Where can they start? In the case illustration about Marcia, the counselor asked her what she wanted to work on first, and then made some suggestions of his own. The client must ultimately make the decision. The social minister should enable the client to search out the alternatives and to make choices based upon a clear understanding of possible consequences. Since the minister is outside the situation, he or she should be able to see things more objectively and thus more clearly.

It is useful for the social minister to take the information gathered in the initial interview and the intake form and to formulate goals that will help in working with the client. These goals should reflect knowledge of the level of functioning in each of the areas of life (domains of living) and the obstacles to functioning in each of these areas. Then the social minister should specify where change must take place first and what else must be given attention at the same time.

In the case of Marcia, after the third interview the social minister worked with her to set a goal of resolving her conflicts with her parents, her church, and her feelings about Jimmy. She would also work toward a decision about her baby, employment, and a plan for her future. The minister asked Marcia which, of the problems she had named, she would feel best about working on first. She said that she would probably need to work on her attitude toward her parents because she was dependent upon them at the time. She was able to acknowledge that they were probably doing the best that they could. The level of intervention chosen was C (Conflict Resolving).

Implementation of Intervention Strategies: Achieving Goals

Once the goals and objectives have been agreed upon by the client and the minister, it is then the task of each to implement the actions that will accomplish the objectives. These actions will lead to achieving the goal. If they are written in behaviorally specific terms, it is easy to know when they have been achieved. Well-formulated goals and objectives are essential to maintaining an effective intervention with a client system.[16]

> With Marcia's permission, her parents were brought into the counseling sessions. Using a family therapy approach, the minister helped to uncover and resolve other major relationship issues. He knew of a center where several pregnant women went for recreation and sharing, and asked if Marcia would like to give it a try. She reluctantly agreed to visit and also to continue coming to the counseling center with her parents for a few weeks.

---

[16]Ibid., 83-90.

As the minister encounters the client at each session it is important that the goal and objectives be flexible enough to change with any new development in the client's situation. Information gathering, problem assessment, and strategy planning continue through the implementation process all the way to termination.

> When Marcia came back the next week she appeared to feel much better. She joked and laughed more than she had the week before. She had gone to the recreation program and made friends with one of the women. She and her mother had talked, and she felt that the "air had cleared somewhat."

> She was still worried about getting a job. Who would hire a pregnant woman? The counselor asked her what kind of a job she wanted. She said she didn't know. She had gone to college to study art, and she loved flower arranging. At the counselor's suggestion, they began to look through the yellow pages of the telephone book. They found a listing for a florist who offered training classes.

> They decided that she would discuss her feelings about Jimmy and her values in the next session. The counselor's goal was to work with her to find a solution to her employment problem and to encourage her to talk through her hostility and clarify her values. In order to solve the employment problem, she needed training, so that had to come first.

It is always good to have a specific objective to accomplish in every session and to define another objective to accomplish between sessions.

> During the week following Marcia's visit the counselor called several florists and found one that would train her, pay her for working part-time until she completed the course, and take her on, knowing that she was pregnant. He immediately called Marcia and suggested that if she was interested, she could call the florist. Marcia called back later in the week to change her appointment because she had gotten the job and enrolled in the training course.

> When she came in for her appointment, she was able to talk through her feelings about Jimmy and her parents. She no longer felt hostility for Jimmy, and she felt that she understood her parents better now. She and her parents

had been talking more, and she had begun to read the Bible and pray in her room before going to sleep at night. She did not feel that her parents were totally correct in their rigidity, but she could accept the fact that they loved her.

In the next session she is to discuss the baby and its future. She has narrowed her choices to keeping the baby or putting it up for adoption.

Implementation of Intervention Strategies: Using Resources

The Social Minister. The church has many resources, including the social minister (or any staff persons who perform ministry). Helping is a person-to-person process, and the helper is always the chief resource. In the case illustration just concluded, the social minister took the initiative to find employment and training opportunities for Marcia. It was up to Marcia to take the initiative at that point and make an appointment with the florist.

Loving and Gifted People. The church is full of loving and gifted people with many skills and talents. These people are often not used in the Lord's service because they are not teachers or singers. So many more persons could be involved in the church's ministries if church staffs would make an effort to find out what each member can do. The staff could then match persons up with a ministry program that would enable them to experience the blessings that come with service.

A man in El Paso did not feel that he was any good at teaching a Sunday School class. He worked with his hands and enjoyed mechanics. But he loved working with boys; his son had been killed in military service.

He was asked to teach a class for younger adolescent boys, but he was a disaster in the classroom. All he knew to do was to read the Sunday School quarterly to them. Nearly all of them quit coming to Sunday School and began hanging out at a local motorcycle shop.

The teacher decided to meet the boys at the shop, where he started a motorbike club that met at the garage every Sunday afternoon. He has reached many of these boys for the Lord and guided them in understanding the Christian

136

life. While he did not teach Sunday School lessons, he did have them start reading and memorizing the Bible.

Many of them, have since grown up and are now active in their church. The motorbike club is still functioning as an alternative to the Sunday School class for boys (and now some girls) who would not attend church.

Facilities. Many of our buildings are unused during the week, and they could be used to help persons. The buildings are generally dedicated to serving the Lord; what better use could be made of this floor space than in His service every day of the week? After-school tutoring groups could be initiated for children who are experiencing difficulty in school. Literacy classes could be offered to adult non-readers. English as a second language could be offered for immigrants whose native language is something other than English. Parenting classes and family financial management classes could be held. Various self-help and other types of support groups could use the educational space for meetings.

Financial Resources. The church has financial resources that could be designated to assist persons in need. Almost anything any organization does will require financial resources. Even if the church adopts a policy that no money will be given to persons who ask for help, finances will be required for other tangible means of ministry. Some churches designate the "plate offerings" on the fifth Sunday of each quarter to benevolence. Others include benevolence in the regular budget.

Visibility. People will come to the church because they know where it is. Historically, persons have thought of churches first when they need mental, emotional, and physical help, since churches have traditionally been places where needy people have found help. Surveys indicate that more than 60 percent of the people in America still think first of the church when help is needed.

Community Resources. For those who are sick, there are doctors and hospitals. For those in trouble with the law, there are lawyers. For those who need psychiatric care, there are psychiatric hospitals and wards at the local hospitals. There are housing authorities to help with shelter. Educational systems provide such resources as adult basic education, vocational retraining, and literacy training. There are usually several agencies that deal with problems associated with each of the domains of living. Most communities have a community social- service resource directory. These are often compiled and managed by a local United Way office. In almost any community, the yellow pages of the telephone directory will contain listings for local and regional service agencies.

Occasionally, church leaders speak distrustfully of these agencies for a variety of reasons. Getting to know persons in these agencies, however, can help assuage anxieties about the viability of referral to them. The social ministers should get to know specific persons at each of these agencies and know exactly how to refer to each. Most social-service agency workers will be overjoyed to work with ministers. They feel that they have a common cause. Some of these workers may be members of the church. They are very happy to see their church become involved.

> As Marcia continued to come for counseling, she seemed to be able to deal with everything but what to do with the baby when it was born. The counselor asked if she would like to talk to a caseworker from the maternity home in the city. She would be under no obligation, but it might help if a professional in dealing with this issue talked with her. The counselor knew that the caseworker was a member of the church and worked in the Preschool Division during extended sessions. Marcia agreed to go the next week and talk with the woman.
>
> She found that she could enter support-group sessions and have individual counseling at the home, where she could explore her options more fully. Marcia and the counselor agreed that this seemed to be the most appropriate thing to do. The counseling relationship was terminated at the church, and Marcia was referred to the maternity home, where she eventually put her child up for adoption.

Termination and Evaluation of Intervention

A part of the termination process is evaluation. This should be done by the minister and the client together.[17] What has happened? What still needs to be done, and how should it be done? An aftercare program may need to be established. The minister's availability for further counseling needs to be discussed. On the nearby conceptual matrix, progress is shown by the arrows. The X's indicate where the client began. There is an X for each assessment and an arrow showing how much progress has been made.

---

[17]Ibid., 90-95.

When the social minister evaluated the intervention with Marcia, he determined that her personal limitations began at functioning level IV-2 and moved to level II-2; her environment was at functioning level III-1 and moved to II-1; a Problem Solving intervention was undertaken when Marcia received training. Her need for training was at functioning level III-2, and it moved to level II-1. Marcia's conflicts with Jimmy began at level functioning level IV-3 and moved to level II-3, with a Conflict Resolving intervention. Her conflicts with her parents began at functioning level IV-2 and moved to level II-2, with a Conflict Resolving intervention. Following a Problem Solving and Conflict Resolving intervention, Marcia's problem with the baby began at level III-3 and moved to level II-2.

The social minister should consider the amount of effort (resources, time, energy) that went into helping each client. It would also be helpful to evaluate the effectiveness of each action. Did it accomplish what it should have accomplished? Would it have been different—better or worse—if another approach had been used? How efficient was the process? Could it have been just as effective with less effort or a different approach? Given the same type of case in the future, would the minister follow a similar procedure?

Termination of an effort should always be done with the client's concurrence unless the client is incapable of making that type of decision. However, ministers should guard against dependency when the client is extremely afraid of terminating the relationship. This is a part of the termination skill that must be developed with experience. Experienced ministers learn to gradually pull everything together so that there is nothing left undone to achieve the goals of the interventions. Clients are made aware of each completion at the appropriate junctures in the intervention process, so that the final termination is not a shock to them. Clients are expecting the helping effort to end, and they are prepared for it, even if they have some lingering inhibitions. The promise of availability will soften the process for the client.

Intervention Tools

Understanding Human Behavior as an Intervention Tool

God has enabled human beings to develop ways of understanding each other. For example, language is built upon this under

	STATUS OF CLIENT SYSTEM FUNCTIONING														
	High-Level Wellness			Well-Being			Mild or Early Dysfunction			Acute Dysfunction			Chronic Dysfunction		
	Well-Being			Stress			Problem			Crisis			Dysfunction		
Cause of Dysfunction	I			II			III			IV			V		
	1	2	3	1	2	3	1	2	3	1	2	3	1	2	3
Personal Limitations				<--------------------------------X											
Environmental Deficiencies				<-------------X											
Policies, Laws, Rules, Regs.															
Catastrophes															
Strategy of Intervention															
Needs (A) Providing															
Problem (B) Solving			<-----training-----X												
				<------baby----------X											
Conflict (C) Resolving				<----------------Jimmy----------X											
			<-------parents------------------X												
System Change															
No Intervention															

140

standing. In their preparation for practice, social ministers need to study the biological, psychological, and social development of human beings in order to understand their needs at various stages of life. Intervening with older persons, for example, is significantly different from intervening with young adults.

Social ministers also need training in cultural variations in human behavior in order to understand how persons of different races and ethnic groups respond to interpersonal, intrapersonal, and environmental problems. For example, Anglo-Americans generally find it easier to discuss personal problems with a professional counselor than do Hispanic persons. Social ministers who are not Hispanic may find it difficult to intervene with Hispanic families. In such cases, referral to Hispanic counselors could be the intervention of choice. If the Anglo-American social ministers speak Spanish and demonstrate understanding and appreciation for Hispanic culture, they may be able to overcome the cultural barrier and provide effective help to the Hispanic family.

Faith as an Intervention Tool

No intervention will be effective unless social ministers and their clients have faith that things will be better. It is essential that social ministers demonstrate an abiding belief in a positive outcome to the intervention. Clients must also possess hope that by accepting help, things will be better for them. Larry Renetzky stated that there is a power within a person's life that gives meaning, purpose, fulfillment, and a will to live. This power lives in everyone, regardless of their theological preference or lack of it. The more persons are tuned in to this "power beyond themselves," the greater their spiritual, physical, psychological, and social well-being.[18] The trigger mechanism that activates this power is faith.

Even when clients seem unable to exercise faith, it is the duty of social ministers to continue believing. This belief is both in the capacity of the client and in God's ability to accomplish his purpose in the client's life.

Prayer as an Intervention Tool

For social ministers, prayer must be an integral part of every intervention. Sometimes, when it is appropriate, this means praying with clients. It is inconceivable, however, that there would ever

---

[18]Larry Renetsky, "The Fourth Dimension: Applications to the Social Services," *Social Work and Christianity*, 14 (Fall 1977), 104.

be a time when praying for clients would be inappropriate. The incarnational nature of social ministers indicates that constant contact with God is essential. However, it is not an innate quality; praying for and with clients does not seem to happen as naturally as breathing. Therefore, praying is a skill to be learned and used in social ministry interventions.

> Ken, the Church and Community Minister at Immanuel Baptist Church, was fresh out of seminary. He wanted to get his practice started in the community "on his best professional foot." He was reluctant to mention faith or to pray with his clients. One day while counseling with a recovering alcoholic, he was about to end a counseling session when the alcoholic asked him,"Brother Ken, why don't we ever pray during our counseling sessions?"

> Ken was embarrassed. He had been struggling with this question for some time. He had concluded, however, that praying during a counseling session would be perceived as unprofessional. The alcoholic went on. "I came to the church for counseling because, in AA, I came to realize that I needed a power greater than myself to help me with my problems. I can get counseling anywhere, but I wanted spiritual counseling as well as regular counseling."

> Ken's heart was broken as he began to pray and confess that he had allowed his professional pride to stand in the way of his commitment to be a holistic minister who was not afraid to include God in everything he did. Ken thanked God for sending this counselee to help him resolve this issue.

> He and this client continue to meet for regular counseling sessions. Now, however, they may begin with prayer; they may end with prayer; or they may pray in the middle of the session. Ken does not always pray with a client. He does, however, always pray for his clients.

The primary purpose of prayer with and for clients is to maintain contact with God, the ultimate social minister, for the benefit of clients and social ministers alike. When prayer comes at the beginning of a session, it invokes the presence of the Holy Spirit and God's wisdom regarding what will be said and done. When it comes during a session, it enables clients and social ministers to deal with issues that call for special divine guidance. When prayer comes at the end of a session, it can sum up what has been discussed and make firm the commitment of clients to take appropriate action regarding their problems.

Although prayer is an essential skill to be used by social ministers, it is not a substitute for other effective intervention skills. It is not appropriate to simply say to a person in need of help, "Pray about it and it will be all right." Sometimes praying about a matter may be all that can be done. Circumstances surrounding a dysfunctional condition may be so great that only God can do anything about them. Most of the time, however, the implementation of proven skills of intervention plus prayer is required for effective help. Effective social ministers will prayerfully use the best skills available in order to meet their clients' needs.

The Bible as an Intervention Tool

Social ministers who "beat their clients over the head with the Bible" may be abusing them rather than helping them. However, the Word of God is a powerful tool when used appropriately. The apostle Paul, in writing to Timothy, stated that the purpose of Scripture is to teach, rebuke, correct, and train in righteousness (2 Tim. 3:16-17). In order to use the Bible as a tool, social ministers must study it constantly.

Some clients may not have been brought up in an environment where moral and ethical values were taught. The Scriptures contain essential guidelines for understanding what moral and ethical living is and how it is to be accomplished. Biblically based instructional materials can be very useful to such clients. Ministers do not have to "shove the Bible down the client's throat" in order to use such materials. Most persons who come to the church or a church-related agency for help expect to hear about God and receive religiously oriented instructions. When biblical materials are used, they can engender faith in clients (Rom. 10:17).

When clients entertain incorrect or destructive notions about life or relationships, the Bible can serve as an authoritative reference. It is the standard by which all ideas and theories are judged. If, for example, a couple wants to live in "an arrangement" rather than get married, the Bible is the authoritative reference to the fact that God does not approve of such arrangements. Social ministers should be able to locate Bible passages that speak to such matters.

Summary and Conclusions

In this chapter we have identified six methods of intervention practiced by social ministers. They are: working with individuals, working with couples, working with families, working with groups, working with organizations, and working with communities.

Five intervention skills were also discussed: (1) information gathering, which includes observing, interviewing, surveying and researching; (2) assessment, which includes determining the levels of client functioning and the obstacles to functioning; (3) intervention strategy planning, which includes goals and objectives, selection of obstacle(s) to functioning with which to intervene, and selection of the range of problems with which to intervene; (4) implementation of intervention strategy; (5) termination and evaluation.

Tools used by Christian social ministers were discussed. These include knowledge of human behavior, faith, prayer, and the Bible.

This chapter is not intended to be a comprehensive discussion of methods and practice. By design it is an overview of the methods, skills, and tools used by social ministers.

Exercises for Review and Examination

1. Write a one-page discussion of each method of social ministry practice listed in this chapter.

2. List and write a paragraph on each of the skills for social ministry.

3. Describe the Watkins-Levine matrix, which was introduced in this chapter. It has three parts. List and describe the use of each part in the process of assessment.

Chapter Seven

Christian Social Minister Roles

Goal: A study of this chapter should enable the social minister to understand the various roles performed in the practice of social ministry.

Objectives: The minister . . .
1. lists the various roles required for the practice of social ministers.
2. describes how and when each role is performed.
3. delineates the specific actions required of each role.

Social ministers are often called upon to perform different roles with different client systems. With individuals, couples, and families, for example, social ministers may function as counselors or case managers. With groups, social ministers may serve as teachers, trainers, planners, advocates, or therapists. With organizations and communities, social ministers may serve as planners, organizers, advocates, or consultants. Most will be generalists. In inner-city mission centers, social ministers may perform as pastor-directors.

Case Manager

One of the most productive roles for the social minister is that of case manager. This role is very similar to the broker role in professional social work.[1] A case manager seeks to aid the client

---
[1]Ronda S. Connaway and Martha E. Gebtry, *Social Work Practice* (Englewood Cliffs: Prentice-Hall, 1988), 60-77.

system in finding, linking with, and making productive use of all the services required to achieve high-level wellness. After determining the problems of functioning and the services needed to alleviate perceived dysfunctions, the case manager will link the client with a number of helping systems in the church, neighborhood, and/or community. Case managers track the client system's progress through the various systems and remain available to client systems throughout the process.

Case managers use all of the skills discussed in chapter 6. Generally, case managers are aggressive in helping client systems find resources for the resolution of their dysfunctional conditions. However, they must guard against creating client system dependency. A rule of thumb is to avoid doing anything for clients that they can do for themselves.

> Aubrey, a Community Minister on the staff of a large inner-city church, interviewed the Jacobson family, who were experiencing difficulty with the utility company. Mr. Jacobson worked at a local defense industry plant and had been laid off. Mrs. Jacobson believed strongly that her job was to stay home and raise their four children. They attended a Holiness church in the community. Many persons at the church had indicated that they were praying for the Jacobsons, but there did not appear to be any let-up in the job situation.

> There were many jobs listed in the paper, but none of them paid as much as Mr. Jacobson's unemployment check. Therefore, he had lost hope of finding suitable employment. The telephone company had recently shut their telephone service off. The electric company was threatening to do the same. They were afraid that the water would soon be shut off and the mortgage company would foreclose if something didn't happen very soon.

> Aubrey discovered that Mr. Jacobson was continuing to collect an unemployment check which amounted to nearly 70 percent of his previous take-home pay. Mr. and Mrs. Jacobson had bought a two-week time-share in a Colorado resort two months after Mr. Jacobson had been laid off, for which they were paying nearly five hundred dollars per month. The Community Minister also found that the family was paying on a ski-boat rig. Mr. Jacobson was making payments on a conversion van, a one-year-

old truck, and an off-road motorcycle. He had three credit cards, each with a five-thousand-dollar limit, which were charged to the maximum.

The social minister suggested that the Jacobsons consider selling everything that was not essential to their survival. They agreed, but wanted Aubrey to take charge of the liquidation sale for them. He refused, but gave them the number of a consumer credit counseling organization which specializes in helping families with problems such as theirs. He also helped them to enroll in a Christian family financial management class that was conducted at the church. A lawyer, a banker, and a CPA were conducting the classes on Sunday evenings.

Aubrey continued to track the Jacobsons progress and gave them constant encouragement to work through their problems until their dysfunctional condition had become one of well-being. Mr. Jacobson was not able to find a job that paid as much as he was making previously. However, with better money management skills he was able to reduce his financial stress to the point that the family appeared to be managing well.

One of the most important skills the effective case manager will use is called networking. Social ministers need to be constantly working to establish reciprocal relationships with service-providing agencies (public, private, and sectarian). They need to become acquainted with the personnel in each of these agencies so that when a client system needs a specific service, the case manager will be able to contact a specific person in an appropriate agency. These relationships can be invaluable. In a reciprocal manner, the personnel in these agencies can contact social ministers and access the help they need to provide for agency clients.[2]

Counselor/Therapist

A social minister who has professional social work training (either a master's degree from a seminary with a concentration or major in social work or a master's degree in social work from a university) will have a significant amount of training in counseling.

---

[2]Lynne Clemmons Morris, "The Circuit Riding Administrator: A Network Based, Macro Generalists' Approach to Capacity Building in Small Communities," *Strategies of Community Organization*, ed. Fred M. Cox and others (Itasca, Ill.: F. E. Peacock Publishers, 1987), 473-486.

The basic skills in social casework are also the basic skills in counseling and psychotherapy. The social minister who functions as a counselor will use the skills of information gathering (family/social history), assessment, intervention strategy planning, strategy implementation, evaluation, and termination. The social minister counselor may work with individuals, couples, families, or groups. Most counseling will be done in an office; however, some of the most effective counseling may be done in the home of the client system.

> Sandra received a Master of Arts degree from the seminary and an M.S.S.W. degree from a state university. She began to work with Mason Street Church as a bivocational community minister while she earned her living as a therapist on the staff of a local psychiatric treatment hospital.
>
> It soon became evident that she would have more work to do at the church if she had the time. At the urging of the church leadership, she changed her status at the hospital and began doing contract work with them. The church was able to provide a small salary, and soon much of Sandra's time was taken up by clients who called the church for help with personal, marital, family, substance abuse, and other problems.
>
> Because Sandra was both a certified social worker and a licensed professional family therapist, she was able to bill the client's insurance for part of the budget for the counseling services provided through the church. The church was able to make up the difference for those who couldn't pay. This enabled Sandra to be a full-time social minister counselor at Mason Street Church.
>
> Much of her family counseling was done in the homes of couples and families rather than at the church building. This was especially helpful when persons felt uneasy about being seen going into the counselor's office at the church.

Educator/Trainer

By design, the case manager and the counselor, must deal with treatment. Generally, they will not be called upon for help until there is a crisis or other form of dysfunction in the client system. It is a common saying among ministers and mental health professionals that we should be about the business of preventing problems before they reach a severely dysfunctional condition. For the social minister, the educator/trainer role provides an effective vehicle for preventive intervention.

Family financial management, drug and alcohol education, AIDS education and awareness, couple and family communication programs, marriage and family enrichment programs, retirement planning, relationship training for senior adults with their adult children, and training adult children for making difficult decisions with their aging parents are just a few of the programs that may be used by the social minister in the educator/trainer role.

Eric, a new social minister on the staff of the Wedgemont Baptist Association, surveyed the churches in the association to discover the needs as perceived by the churches to whom he was responsible. Most of the churches indicated that they needed help with dealing with the many transients who came by their churches asking for food, shelter, gasoline, and clothing. Others indicated that they were concerned with the growing drug problems among the youth in their communities. Still others were concerned about the AIDS situation and what their churches might do if they were confronted with the problem.

Eric called a group of pastors together and asked them to help him prioritize the problems. They chose the AIDS problem as the most pressing. Second was the drug and alcohol problem among the youth. The third was the need to have a central tracking system for emergency assistance programs. They agreed that an educational program regarding the HIV virus and the AIDS problem would be helpful to them in establishing church policies for their nursery and preschool departments. They gave Eric the authority to secure the services of some noted specialists from a nearby city to lead a workshop for interested church leaders.

Since Eric was a certified drug and alcohol counselor, he was invited to hold drug and alcohol awareness workshops for parents and teens in several churches during the next year. He also planned and implemented a workshop for church staff members for working with emergency assistance requests. He then enlisted a number of

149

volunteers to staff a program at the Association office for tracking persons who asked for help from any of the cooperating churches.

Advocate

From time to time the social minister will encounter situations in which persons are being hurt by rigid policies, rules, regulations or practices. Often these persons feel that they do not have a voice. They feel that no one will listen to them, or that they do not know how to confront a harmful issue. The social minister is uniquely trained to study the system, determine the best way to change the system, and implement a strategy designed to change a harmful system on behalf of a client. This process is called advocacy.

> Janie, a poorly educated, almost illiterate mother received a monthly SSI check to support her legally blind son. She was constantly coming to the church at about same time each month, asking for help. Sometimes she needed food; sometimes she needed money for a prescription; at other times she needed money to go to the doctor.
>
> Ann, the social minister at the church, visited Janie in her home. Ann found that Janie received enough money to pay the rent and utilities, and enough money was left over to buy groceries and medicine. In addition to the SSI check, she also received a Social Security check. She was eligible to purchase food stamps and to receive government surplus commodities. She could also get Medicaid payments to help with the prescriptions and doctor's bills.
>
> Ann called a caseworker at the food stamp office and discovered that a supervisor had become angry with Janie and refused to renew her application. The same thing had happened at the SSI office. Ann called the supervisors at each of the offices and made an appointment to bring Janie in to see them. She was able to convince the supervisors to review Janie's case and to reinstate her eligibility.
>
> Ann then assigned a social work student to work with Janie, helping her learn some money-management skills so that her income would cover her needs.

Social Planner

As social ministers work with congregations, neighborhoods, special groups, and organizations in the community, the role of planner becomes very important. A planner helps groups and organizations to assess their problems, determine the obstacles to their functioning, develop action strategies for removing the obstacles, and implement those strategies. Sometimes the social ministry planners work to empower people to find solutions to their own problems. Planners work to enable indigenous leaders to keep the people in the community, organization, or group on target. At other times they may serve as community therapists, helping factions in the community or organization to resolve conflicts and unify for the purpose of resolving a problem. In other situations, planners may become social activists, organizing people to make dramatic changes in systems.

Greg, a social minister and director of an inner-city mission center, became disturbed by the callous way the county commissioner was treating the people of a housing project that was served by the center. The center had sponsored a voter registration drive in the projects before the last elections. Their votes had elected the commissioner.

Streets and streetlights in the area in and around the project were in bad repair. Over half of the lights had been out for over two months. Streets in other sections near the center had been repaired, but the ones directly adjacent to the project were in poor condition. People were afraid to venture out at night because of the darkness.

Greg invited all of the registered voters and other concerned persons to come to the center to determine what might be done. The commissioner was invited, but declined to attend. This angered the residents. Greg suggested that they construct a resolution, asking the commissioner to intervene on their behalf. It was signed by all of the registered voters in the area. Still, the commissioner refused to even talk with them.

Greg then gathered the voters together and attended the next county commissioners' meeting. He also contacted the local newspaper, radio stations, and television stations. While standing outside the county courthouse he was asked to make a statement to the television audience. He told of the problem and indicated that the commissioner had not even responded to their resolution. The commissioner was then asked to respond. He had nothing to say but the next week the streetlights were repaired and a crew began working on the potholes in the streets.

Consultant

Often social ministers are employed by denominational agencies as advisers to churches or judicatories. They are called in to help with some problem or to enable a congregation or association to develop a program of ministry. Some social ministers may serve as private consultants to churches, judicatories, or agencies. The role of consultant generally takes on one or more of the following forms:

1. *Client-centered case consultation.* This role is one in which the social minister is asked to consult with another worker regarding the needs of a client system. The consultant will help the worker to understand the specific problems faced by the client system and which strategies might be most appropriate for the relief of the client system's dysfunction.

2. *Worker-centered case consultation.* In this situation the focus is on the worker and his or her practice skills regarding interventions with client systems.

3. *Organization-centered management consultation.* Here the role of the social minister consultant is to assist the administrator of an organization (church, association, agency) with assessment and planning for the improvement of organizational functioning and/or the correction of an organizational dysfunction.

4. *Management-centered organizational consultation.*[3] In this situation, the social minister has been called in to evaluate and make suggestions regarding the performance of the administrator and/or staff.

Market Street Church called upon the community minister at First Church to come and study their situation and to make recommendations regarding how the Market Street Church might improve its outreach to its surrounding neighborhood. Jackson, the community minister at

[3]Derrel Watkins, "Social Work Consultation and the Church," *Church Social Work*, ed. Diana S. Richmond Garland (St. Davids, Penn.: North American Association of Christians in Social Work, 1992), 17-35.

First Church, arranged to look over the records of Market Street Church and led the staff to study the demographic data regarding their neighborhood.

A profile of the community revealed that the neighborhood had changed from mostly single-family dwellings to mostly multi-family dwellings. Most households in the community were occupied by renters. The school records revealed that a significant number of families moved in and out of the area each semester. The African-American and Hispanic-American population had each risen by 10 percent during the past decade. There continued to be a large number of older persons living in owner-occupied single-family dwellings.

Market Street Church wanted to reorganize their ministry and outreach program and adapt to the new community profile. Five years ago, First Church had experienced the same type of phenomenon. The community minister had both an academic and experiential knowledge of the process. He was able to assist Market Street to develop new programs, enlarge its staff to include ethnic representation, and adapt its worship style to meet the needs of the new residents while also meeting the needs of the older members of the congregation and community. He was able to use all four models of consultation in his role as consultant.

Evangelist

Social ministers work at maintaining a balance in the types of evangelism used in social ministry. *Confrontational evangelism* is used when assessment reveals that persons do not have a saving relationship with Jesus Christ. Social ministers, along with other members of the staff and congregation, may engage in door-to-door visitation. Some social ministers have been put in charge of the evangelistic outreach programs of their church or judicatory. There are times when social ministers introduce Christ to persons who come to their offices or centers for other types of help.

Life-style evangelism is also an important aspect of the life and witness of social ministers. Social ministers not only "talk the talk," but they "walk the walk" of the Christian. This includes consistent attitudes and acts of Christlike acceptance of persons in need as well as living a life characterized by Christian moral ethics.

Demonstration evangelism is another expression of social ministers' witness. It is intentional and sensitive to the spiritual needs of client systems—intentional in that social ministers make sure that clients know that the help given is in the name of Christ, and sensitive in that no attempt is made to pressure persons into making professions of faith. Persons must not be pressured to make a false profession simply to please helpers, but it is equally important that social ministers not avoid leading persons to Christ out of the fear of creating "rice Christians." Social ministers can rely upon the Holy Spirit to provide wisdom in such circumstances.

Generalists

Most social ministers on church or judicatory staffs are generalists by necessity. That is, they may be required to perform many roles. The specific roles that ministers perform at any given time depend on the needs brought to them by client systems. Generalists are prepared to be counselors to individuals, couples, families, and groups who are seeking help with some interpersonal or intrapersonal problem. Generalists regularly serve as educators/trainers, even if that is not considered their primary role. Often generalists are called on to help clients deal with dysfunctional systems and to play the role of advocate. At other times social ministers are planners and consultants. As *Christian* social ministers they perform the role of evangelist. Finally, the primary role of generalists is that of case manager, in which they are linked to many relevant systems in churches, judicatories, and community agencies.

Pastor/Director

Mission centers are rapidly replacing community centers as the strategic locations for ministry and evangelism in the inner city. As this phenomenon increases social ministers are being called upon to serve as pastors of church-type missions while also directing community weekday ministries. This means that social ministers need training in such pastoral duties as preaching, worship planning, church organization, educational program administration, and performing weddings and funerals, along with the skills of counseling and other forms of intervention they already possess.

> Jerry had graduated from the seminary and the school of social work. For a number of years he had been serving as the director of a community center located adjacent to a

large government housing project. He was content with his role as the director which allowed him to exercise all of his social work skills.

The agency which supported the center decided that the people who were being served through the center needed to have a church-mission which could meet their worship as well as their social needs. At first Jerry was very disappointed. He felt that the arrangement they had with a nearby church was meeting the needs of persons who wanted to attend worship services.

He had not thought about being a pastor, but the more he prayed about it the more he felt that this was what God wanted him to do. He accepted the responsibility for starting the mission church in the community center.

Within a short time a full-fledged church-type mission was established with worship services three times each week. They had Sunday School for all ages, discipleship training, and mission education organizations. Volunteers from several large churches in the city helped to staff the organizations until local persons could be trained to fill most of the offices of the church.

During the past year Jerry has performed six weddings and ten funerals. He is now called "Preacher" by the local residents. In every way he is still a social worker, but he is also a pastor. For Jerry, it is a natural progression in his spiritual pilgrimage.

Missionary

Social ministry programs are not strangers to mission strategy. However, the role of the social minister has not always been clear in the minds of foreign mission boards. Some missionary positions are specifically social work oriented. These, however, are few and often a source of confusion to other missionaries. The Foreign Mission Board of the Southern Baptist Convention has stated that seminary-trained social ministers who have taken courses in theology, missions, evangelism, religious education, and church administration along with their social work courses may be uniquely prepared to serve as church developers on a number of mission fields. In this capacity they would use their knowledge of the organization and functioning of churches to aid indigenous churches in the host country with organizational development, evangelism and church growth. In addition, these social ministry missionaries would help by organizing persons to reach out to the community through weekday ministry programs.

One skill essential to the social ministry missionary is contextualization. This should be taught to all students, regardless of which roles they may perform. Contextualization refers to the process of adapting both the missionary message and the methods to the understanding and needs of the people of another culture. It is the process of bridging the gap between the social minister and the client system for the purpose of maximizing the effect of an intervention.[4]

Contextualization does not imply, however, that the biblical truth must be watered down. Rather, on the contrary, effective contextualization requires that persons from both cultures subscribe to a standard and work together in a collaborative effort to understand each other and to understand the message. Along with the message, the social minister needs to learn from the host culture which types of intervention may be most effective.[5]

> When Melody was appointed to work with Mexican-Americans, she had no idea of what she was getting into. She was ambivalent regarding the place the State Missions Department had sent her. The only Latin Americans she had ever known were two girls who had attended Ouachita Baptist University in Arkansas. She had sat next to one of them in a couple of classes. She had, however, been told about the Latin American culture in a new missionary orientation and training retreat.
>
> Fortunately, Melody had taken a course in human behavior in which the principles of contextualization had been discussed. During her first few weeks on the field, she saw people do things that made no sense to her. Some of the language caused her to blush. It soon became so commonplace that she hardly noticed. She found it difficult to believe that people could live in the poverty-based conditions she saw in community after community along the river. She also developed an appreciation and love for the people. They also began to express appreciation and respect for her.

---

[4]See a discussion about this skill in James W. Green, *Cultural Awareness in the Human Services* (Englewood Cliffs: Prentice-Hall, 1982), 6-27.

[5]Paul G. Hiebert, *Anthropological Insights for Missionaries* (Grand Rapids: Baker Book House, 1987), 171-179.

She secured the services of a Mexican-American teenage girl to translate for her. She also found a Mexican-American schoolteacher who was willing to tutor her in Spanish. Two semesters of Spanish in college had not prepared her to communicate fluently. These two helpers taught Melody much about the local customs and about the Hispanic culture.

She soon learned that the books on counseling methods and social work practice that she had brought with her were useless. Everything she had learned had to be adapted to the unique features of the culture in which she was now serving. For example, she quickly saw the folly of setting up an office and expecting people to come in and talk about their problems. Her training in family therapy helped her to assess the relationship problems she observed, but she found that the most effective approach to solving family problems was to encourage the extended family system to help the couple work through their problems.

She had always been a stickler for being on time. She would get upset when anybody was late for an appointment or when a Sunday School class didn't start on time. Melody soon learned to forget the clock. People would assemble when they got there and leave when they were ready. They would keep appointments when they showed up. Complaining would only alienate the persons she was trying to help. Her program planning had to take on this quality of flexibility, and she eventually learned to relax and work with the people according to their cultural traits rather than her own.

Administrator

Eventually, most social ministers will be called upon to manage ministry programs. This function calls for skills in decision-making, organizational development, planning, supervising, and evaluating programs. Social ministry administrators must also develop skills in fund-raising, budgeting, and public relations.

When Ross entered seminary and later the graduate school of social work, he thought that he would become a family therapist. Being an administrator was the furthest thing from his thinking. His academic adviser suggested that he take as many administration courses as he could work into his curriculum. "You will soon be an administrator," his advisor said. "It doesn't matter what your major is. As a graduate social worker and a minister, you will be asked to be in charge of a program somewhere."

The adviser was correct. Immediately upon graduation, Ross was offered a position as director of social ministry programs in a large city. Yes, he would use his skills in family counseling, but he would also be the supervisor of a staff of social ministers in two community centers. Fortunately, he had taken two courses in human service administration at the university and two courses in church and education administration at the seminary. These courses in church administration were very valuable, since he was working for an association of churches.

Summary and Conclusions

A few social ministers serve in unidimensional positions that require them to perform only one role to fulfill their duties. Most social ministers, however, are generalists. For this reason social ministry training is multidimensional. Social ministry as well as professional social work curricula is varied to prepare social ministers for this diversity. Social ministers and social workers must understand psychology, sociology, economics, management, political science, and the biological sciences. Their counseling skills are similar to those of counseling psychologists. Their research skills are similar to those of sociologists. They must be competent administrators. They must know and understand public policy issues and the functioning of political systems. In addition, they must have a basic understanding of the physical needs of persons.

Exercises for Review and Examination

1. Define and briefly discuss the role of case manager.
2. How is the role of case manager different from that of generalist? Please explain.
3. How do the roles of evangelist and missionary differ? How are they alike?
4. Are the roles of pastor and social minister in conflict? Explain your response.

Chapter Eight

Programming for Social Ministry

Goal: A study of this chapter should enable the social minister to understand the basic process of programming for social ministry.

Objectives: The minister . . .

1. discusses the need for program focus in social ministry programs.
2. describes the essential differences among enrichment, prevention, and treatment programs in social ministry.
3. outlines the steps in program planning.
4. describes six administrative guidelines for social ministry programs.

Focus in Social Ministry Programming

Congregations and judicatories often make the mistake of copying programs that work in other communities or congregations, without considering whether the program is suited for them. Certain aspects of the program may be easily adapted to their specific community, but all programs need to be evaluated in light of their unique characteristics and how they may function in a specific environment. It would be useful for each entity to apply the "AAA" rule of thumb: first, *acquire* the model; second, *adapt* the model to the local environment; and third, *apply* the adapted model.

Denominational agencies produce resource guides for congregations and judicatories which may be useful in helping committees or staff persons with planning programs of ministry. However, these guides are not intended for use in every situation. They must be adapted as the unique makeup of a specific church and community dictates.

Goals and objectives of programs should be determined in light of the mission of the church or judicatory. For example, if a particular congregation perceives its only mission as evangelizing the lost in a particular neighborhood, then every program developed must contribute to fulfilling that mission. In that case, the goals and objectives of any ministry program should contain an intentional evangelistic strategy. However, if the mission statement of the church is broader, including ministry as a specific part of the congregation's purpose in addition to evangelism, then the goals and objectives of ministry programs may be less specific regarding its evangelistic role.

Enrichment Programs

Ministry programs are sometimes perceived only as services for dysfunctional persons. But these programs may focus on persons who are experiencing high-level wellness as well. High-level wellness refers to persons who are not experiencing any form of dysfunction in any of their domains of living. The focus of ministry programs for this group is *enrichment*. All persons, regardless of their social, emotional, mental, relational, economic, and spiritual condition, need to continue to grow and enrich their lives. Social ministry programs that meet the needs of persons for enrichment will make use of the same skills as those focusing on dysfunctional persons.

Social ministers who are working with a group of lively, able-bodied older persons, for example, should gather as much information as possible about each member of the group. They should then make an assessment to determine in what specific domains of living the clients would receive the most benefit. Strategy planning involves goals, objectives, and action plans. Finally, the worker should implement and evaluate the enrichment plan with the older persons.

Spiritual Enrichment

Spiritual well-being is difficult to define. Every metaphor one could use is mental, emotional, relational, or physical. In reality, spiritual wellness is an integral part of every aspect of persons' lives. It refers to the celebration of a vital, growing relationship with God in Christ. It involves a deepening understanding of God's revelation of Himself in the Bible. A consistent and meaningful prayer life is also a facet of spiritual well-being. Appreciation of the presence of other human beings and respect for every person's worth, regardless of race, ethnicity, or social status, is a part of spiritual well-being. Celebrating God's creation of the physical environment and its beauty is also important to spiritual well-being.

Emotional Enrichment

Programs that lift the human spirit and enhance one's feelings of self-worth serve those who are already experiencing high-level wellness as well as those who may be dysfunctional in some ways. Poetry, music, drama, travel, sight-seeing, and so on may provide the basis of programs designed to meet the needs of highly functional persons for emotional enrichment.

Mental Enrichment

As long as human beings are healthy and alive, they can learn. Each new fact, concept, skill, or ability that they learn enriches their lives. Bible, church history, world history, American history, government, literature, music, psychology, sociology, gardening, landscaping, languages, art, drama, designing clothes, cooking, parenting, communication skills, relationship building, conflict resolving, education and training skills, nutrition, woodwork, bricklaying, mechanics, electronics, and many other subjects can be the basis of mental enrichment ministries in a church.

Relationship Enrichment

Often persons who are functioning at a state of high-level wellness will enjoy learning how to appreciate other people in more positive ways. This is especially true of husbands and wives and other family members. Retreats and workshops designed to enrich family living can be effective ministries. Conferences on human relations can add to an already enriched life. A study of skills for the development of a sense of community can also be valuable.

Physical Enrichment

A body may be in good condition, but it takes work to keep it that way. Opportunities to study and practice good nutrition and appropriate exercise for a person's age group, condition of health, and body type can enrich the life of one who is already healthy.

Economic Enrichment

If one has enough money to take care of the necessities of life and purchase other desirable items, one could be said to be in a state of economic well-being. Persons can also be enriched economically if they have enough money beyond the tithe to help others who are less fortunate. It is desirable for the person or family to have a plan for economic security. God provides for His children, but He will also provide ways for His servants to earn the money they need for continued life and service. Educational and counseling programs that enable persons to enrich their economic well-being can be a valuable ministry.

Prevention Programs

Persons experiencing significant stress in their lives and those who seem to be struggling just to keep going are probably in need of preventive intervention. That is, they will likely benefit from programs that equip and enable them to move toward a state of high-level wellness. Some persons may be enjoying a condition of well-being, not needing any form of treatment; but they are in need of help to keep their condition from deteriorating into a dysfunctional condition where they will be needing treatment.

Such programs as couple communication, marriage enrichment, family communication, parenting skills training, conflict resolution, job training, career development, employment-seeking skills, support groups for recovering addicts, support groups for children of divorce, support groups for adult children of dysfunctional homes, adult basic education, literacy training, computer skills, classes in cooking and nutrition, recreation and aerobic programs, physical fitness programs, prayer and Bible study fellowships, prisoner re-entry and support programs for released offenders and their families, and personal and family financial planning classes are just a few of the almost limitless possibilities. All of these programs can serve a vital role in the prevention of greater problems.

Most enrichment programs have an educational flavor. The assumption is that if persons know about some potentially dangerous situation or behavior, they can avoid it. This is not always the case. Most addicts, for example, know all of the consequences and dangers of the substances they are abusing. Yet they continue to partake. Many inner-city adolescents who engage in destructive activities are well aware of the dangers. Programs whose goal is to enable adolescents to become strong enough to resist the temptations of the "street society" and encourage them to pursue constructive alternatives could be very helpful.

> Darold was a Christian social minister working for a metropolitan association. He became concerned that the inner-city mission center and churches were ineffective in their efforts to reach and salvage the large numbers of youth who roamed the streets at night. Some of the adolescents had grown up attending the Sunday Schools and Bible clubs offered by the mission center and the churches in their neighborhoods. Now, however, they were committed to the gangs in their communities.

> Some of them talked of wanting to get out, but they did not have the support at home or in the community to make the break. Darold realized that if nothing was done, these adolescents would possibly be killed, go to jail or prison, or become hopeless addicts. He wanted to prevent this from happening.

> Darold called together five pastors of the missions and inner-city churches. With the blessings of his supervisor, he organized two special programs designed to rescue some of these adolescents. One program was an apprenticeship for the boys and girls who had dropped out of school. He found store owners, construction contractors, carpenters, mechanics, janitorial contractors, and a school administrator who were willing to accept these adolescents as apprentices.

> He then went to the adolescents and discussed the apprenticeship program with them. Some were interested and were ready to commit themselves to the program. Most were leery. They had been let down so many times that they did not trust this "gringo." Darold felt that, in time, he could reach some of them.

> The second program the committee designed was a four-week float trip and wilderness jaunt in the mountains and forests along the Buffalo and White rivers of northwest Arkansas. They enlisted a group of young adult men and

women from churches all over the association to help with this program. They secured a foundation grant to fund the jaunt and accepted the donation of a bus and driver from a travel and touring company.

Darold and his helpers spoke with the parents and the adolescents and received the parents' permission for the boys and girls to make the trip. The adolescents (mostly twelve- to fifteen-year-olds) were organized to raise as much of their own support as possible through car washes, can and paper collections and other activities. In this way they would feel that they had some ownership in the program. Only time will tell how effective this preventive intervention program has been.

Treatment Programs

When persons, families, groups and communities become dysfunctional, acutely or chronically, treatment is needed. *Treatment* is used here to refer to a type of help given when the client system requests specific interventions, such as problem-solving or conflict-resolving and/or system change, in order to move from a dysfunctional condition to a state of well-being. A *problem-solving ministry* seeks to equip the client system (individual, family, group, organization, or community) with skills that will enable them to solve their problems. There is an educational or didactic process implied in this type of intervention. Counseling and skills training are the primary approaches of this strategy of intervention.

> Gregory, an African-American male about twenty-five years old, came by the Baptist Mission Center one Monday morning. He was well known by the staff and could call most of them by their first names. He saw Jeff, an assistant director, and said, "Say, Jeff, my man. How about getting me a job? I've been out of work for over a month."
>
> Jeff had taken the initiative to get Gregory his last job. Gregory had been fired after working only three weeks. Jeff never did know why, but the employer had called and told him to be careful about who he recommended in the future. Gregory had told Jeff that the man was racist.
>
> Jeff asked Gregory to step into his office, where he told him that he would not get him another job. He would,

however, suggest that Gregory enter into a new job-seeking skills class that the center would begin on Thursday. He handed Gregory a form to fill out. It was then that he noticed Gregory could not read or write. He was startled because he knew that Gregory had graduated from high school and had attended at least one year of college on an athletic scholarship. Jeff closed the door so that their conversation would be potentially less embarrassing to Gregory. Jeff asked Gregory if he had considered enrolling in adult literacy classes. This seemed to infuriate Gregory. He accused Jeff of being a racist and stormed out of the office.

In the lobby of the center, Gregory ran into a middle-aged African-American who was a volunteer at the center. He began to berate the staff at the center and called them a bunch of racists again. Jeff had followed Gregory to the lobby and saw who he was talking to. Jeff asked the man to tell his story to Gregory. After Gregory settled down, he agreed to listen to the older "brother."

The older man's name was Bobby. He had graduated from college and had played professional football for two years before being injured so severely that he could not play any longer. He found that he could not get a job because he could not read well enough to follow written instructions. Bobby had enrolled in an adult literacy class and was now an instructor for the Adult Basic Education class that met at the center on Thursday evenings.

Gregory agreed to begin the Thursday morning job-seeking skill class when he found that Bobby was teaching it. Bobby was also able to convince Gregory to begin working with a literacy tutor.

Conflict-resolving ministry involves a more clinical approach to intervention. That is, the social minister will employ professional counseling skills, enabling the client system to resolve interpersonal problems or intrapersonal problems. Programs designed to make use of such skills are generally found in counseling or comprehensive family ministry centers.

Red Mountain Association's Director of Missions continued to hear about a need for Christian counseling services. Various stories had been circulated about the damage some secular counselors had done to some individuals and couples in one or two of the churches.

Several pastors had discussed the fact that their counseling loads were becoming so heavy that they could hardly get anything else done. Some indicated that they would love to have a good Christian counselor to refer their people to if one could be found. One problem, however, was that many people who needed this help could not afford the only Christian psychiatric clinic in the area. There was a waiting list, and the fees were very high. With state mission support, the Association had recently called a Director of Christian Social Ministries. Her name was Nancy. She had a Master of Arts degree in Church Social Services from the seminary, and an M.S.S.W. degree from the state university. She was not a licensed counselor, but she did know someone who had graduated with her from the seminary and the university who had specialized in "direct practice," which included marriage and family therapy training.

She found that he had become licensed by the state as a marriage and family therapist and a drug and alcohol abuse counselor; he was also a licensed professional counselor. He was presently working for a Christian psychiatric clinic in another state, but his long-range desire was to work with a group of churches to develop a comprehensive family service program which included professional counseling.

Upon her recommendation, the Director of Missions interviewed the counselor and recommended him to the executive board of the association. The pastors of the association agreed to ask their churches to increase their giving to the association budget so that the counselor could be hired. He would be available to all the churches as an associational staff member.

When the obstacles to functioning involve rigid laws, rules, regulations, or practices, a *system change ministry* may be indicated. Persons are sometimes victims of policies that may be unfair or unfairly implemented by organizations or government agencies. The social minister may choose to use social action and community organization skills in order to confront and change these practices on behalf of the client system.

Bob, a pastor-director of a mission center in a city in the Southwest, heard that a developer was going through the community trying to buy up the houses. The developer even came by the center and asked to whom she might submit a proposal to purchase the center property. She was vague about whom she represented and what the intentions were regarding the property in the area. While most of the houses were old and in need of repair, they were the only housing that most of the residents could afford. There was no other section of the city where property values were as low.

Most of the people in the neighborhood decided that they would not sell. Soon the city began to put pressure on the residents of the neighborhood to clean up their houses, lawns, and sidewalks. Police began to give out tickets to the residents for even small, unintentional infractions. Some of the houses were condemned by the city housing authority. The fire department was very slow to respond to a call from a house in the neighborhood.

Bob's telephone began to ring all day long. People were frantic. They didn't know what to do. A deacon in one of the churches that supported the center was also on the city planning commission. He told his pastor that the area where the mission center was located was targeted for development as a shopping center and high-rise office complexes.

No hearing had been held, and the plans had not been made public. Bob called some of the community leaders together. They decided to make public what they had been experiencing. The deacon on the city planning commission would not make a public statement, but he did give Bob the information about the development company and what their strategy might be.

Bob called a friend on the local newspaper and asked him to do some investigating. An investigative reporter on one of the local television news teams was brought in. When they made the news public about the collusion between the planning commission and the developer, interest in the neighborhood ceased. The people were no longer harassed.

Steps in Developing Ministry Programming

The basic steps for developing ministry programs follow closely the steps in Sunday School growth: discover the possibilities; enlarge the organization; provide the space; enlist and train the workers; and contact the prospects. When a person or group develops programming for social ministry, the steps include: (1) locate and identify the people who have a need; (2) plan to meet specific needs; (3) gather resources and provide a place for the ministry; (4) enlist and train the ministry staff; and (5) implement a strategy of outreach.

Step 1: Locate and Identify the People Who Have a Need

All types of persons in all socioeconomic groups have needs. In reality, regardless of persons' socioeconomic status, their needs are very similar: spiritual, emotional, mental, relational, economic, and physical. Poverty-based persons in the community have spiritual, emotional, relational, and physical needs in addition to economic needs. Lower middle-class persons may not have the same basic economic needs as poverty-based persons, but they may have all of the other needs. Middle-class and upper middle-class persons may not have the same type of economic needs as those in the lower socioeconomic classes, but their needs are similar in other ways. The wealthy may have just as many spiritual, emotional, and relational needs as lower socioeconomic groups.

To a great extent, the location and makeup of the church or center will determine the particular groups and needs of persons for whom programs will be developed. However, before a person or group plans a program, it is important that specific information about the target group be gathered and evaluated. Questions to be answered are: Who (or how many persons) has what specific problem(s), caused by what obstacles to functioning, at what level of severity?

Step 2: Plan to Meet Specific Needs

Social ministry focuses on persons with needs, both real and perceived. *Effective ministry focuses on specific needs.* Persons have spiritual, mental, emotional, relational, and physical needs. Programs should be planned and implemented to meet one or more of these needs. This can be accomplished by focusing on a single need or a combination of needs.

Effective ministry is with persons. This is in contrast to planning and implementing programs for the sake of programming. Persons have needs. It is therefore important that ministry programs address the needs of specific persons. We may consult with groups, neighborhoods, and communities as we plan, but ultimately we must identify specific persons who need our programs of intervention.

Effective ministry must be Christ-centered and empowered by the Holy Spirit. Ministry programs should focus on the teaching and modeling of Christ. All of our planning is in vain unless the program is led and empowered by the Holy Spirit. The Holy Spirit provides wisdom in planning. The Holy Spirit's presence is essential to the effectiveness of the ministry. The Holy Spirit keeps the focus upon Christ and His will for the ministry.

Effective ministry has a definite place in the total life of the church. The church must recognize that organized ministry programs are both biblical and desirable. The level of church support will predetermine the ultimate effectiveness of any ministry program. Social ministers will do well to remember this principle and to begin ministries only after the church has demonstrated a high level of support. The need for support begins with the staff and continues throughout the membership of the congregation or judicatory.

Step 3: Gather Resources and Provide a Place for the Ministry

God's primary plan for funding His work is accomplished by the tithes and offerings of His people. Other sources of funding, such as foundation grants and gifts from organizations, businesses, and individuals, are not in violation of His will, but they are secondary to God's primary will. In any case, adequate funding is essential to a successful program of ministry.

A place (building, room, office) for ministry is a very important resource. Persons need to know where they can go or call in order to receive the help the ministry is designed to provide. The quality of the facility is also very important to the ministry. Any ministry that carries the name of Christ deserves the best the church or center can provide. The most effective ministries are implemented in very attractive surroundings.

Adequate equipment and supplies are also very important aids for ministry planning. Tables, chairs, multisensory aids (tape players, VCRs and video monitors, overhead projectors, movie projectors, chalkboards), paper, pencils, vans and buses, and books are just a few items possibly needed in a ministry program.

Step 4: Enlist and Train the Ministry Staff

Before any ministry program is begun, the staff (both paid and volunteer) should be enlisted and trained for the specific tasks required to implement the program. Even professional social workers will need to be trained or oriented to the specific ministry tasks to be undertaken by the program.

For some tasks, such as work with alcoholics and other chemical abusers, professionals from the community might be enlisted to provide training workshops for the staff. For other programs, training manuals and other training resources may be available from denominational publishing houses and other service agencies. These could be utilized along with consultants in order to adequately prepare the staff for the most effective implementation of the program.

Prayer and Bible study are essential ingredients in the development of the ministry staff. Praying and studying God's Word together can facilitate spiritual bonding among the staff, proving to be the difference between an effective Christ-centered, and Spirit-filled ministry and one that is fragmented and ineffective, although carried out by Christian workers under the auspices of a church or other religious organization.

Step 5: Implement a Strategy of Outreach

It does little good to plan a wonderful ministry if those who need it do not know of its existence. Therefore, advertising is a key component in ministry program strategy. Putting signs in conspicuous places, in language that persons can read and understand, can be a first step in making persons aware of the service. Printed handbills, delivered door to door in the targeted neighborhood, also inform the public. Radio and television ads and newspaper releases can make the general public aware of the ministry. Most local news media personnel will be happy to receive well-written news releases about services designed to help persons in their area. Public announcements of various forms can be effective also.

Another source of outreach is the cultivation of referral networks. Various social service agencies are constantly looking for programs which provide additional services to the persons they are serving. A personal letter to each of these agencies can strengthen the link between the church's social ministry program and the providers of services in other agencies. These agencies can be located by checking the yellow pages of the telephone book or a community services resource book (often published by United Way).

Administrative Guidelines for Programming

There are some basic administrative guidelines which should be adhered to at various stages of developing and administering a program.

1. Decision Making

Some basic questions should be answered before the planning of a program. They include: Does this need call for a new program, or is it already being met by other programs? Could we reorganize an existing program to include this need? Do we have the resources to do anything about this? If not, where will we get the resources? Is this a need that we really want to do something about? Where in the order of priorities does this type of program fall? Who will have specific responsibility for supervising this program? Will that person (or persons) have the time and energy to implement the program? Who should be involved in planning this program? Who will make the final decisions? When do we want to start planning?

2. Planning: Mission, Goals, Specific Objectives

The first phase in planning is determining *the mission of the church or agency* and how it relates to this type of ministry. Mission statements express what the church or agency is trying to accomplish as a result of its nature—its location in a specific environment at a specific time in history.

> Oak Grove Church was located in the middle of a largely agricultural county in a midwestern state. Every summer large numbers of migrant farm laborers came to help with the harvest. Delbert Jones had recently been called to be

the pastor of the church. The congregation was largely made up of families who were related to managing the farms in the area. They were generally faithful in attendance, prayed for missions, gave generously to special mission offerings, and considered themselves to be a typical rural evangelical church.

Delbert's heart went out to the migrant families. He felt that the church should do something to minister to them while they were in the area. He spoke about this concern with an area director of home missions. The director referred him to the state Church and Community Ministries consultant. The Church and Community Ministries consultant readily agreed to assist Delbert in every possible way.

The first question the consultant asked, however, stumped Delbert: "Does your church have a mission statement we could look at?" Delbert didn't know, so he asked the chairman of the deacons. The deacon chairman didn't know either. They didn't have a constitution and by-laws. The deacon could not remember ever discussing a mission statement. He felt that it was the mission of any church to win the lost to Christ.

The consultant suggested that they call the membership together and attempt to come up with a mission statement that the church could adopt. The Bible study program of the church was just finishing a study of the Book of Acts, so Delbert began the meeting by discussing whether the church felt that its mission was the same as the church in the Book of Acts. The membership agreed that it was.

They then came up with the following mission statement: "Understanding that people everywhere need to have a saving relationship with Christ, and recognizing that Christians everywhere are called upon to be His witnesses at home, in the county, the state, the nation and around the world, it is the mission of the Oak Grove Church to endeavor to engage persons in Bible study, worship, evangelism, discipleship, and ministry which is in keeping with the New Testament model of the church."

Delbert brought up the issue of the migrant farm laborers and asked if they fit into the mission of the Oak Grove

Church. With only one or two negative votes, the membership determined that the migrants were a part of their mission responsibility. They were in favor of beginning a ministry with migrant families. The director of the Woman's Missionary Union was appointed as the chairperson of an ad hoc committee to study the needs and bring back a proposal for the church to consider.

Every part of the planning process for a ministry should relate to the mission of the church. When the mission is clearly fixed in the minds of the planners and a decision is made to develop a ministry, the second phase, *goal-setting,* can begin. Goals should reflect the need of the client population (target group) and relate to the purpose and function of the church. Goals should be behaviorally specific. They should state what will be happening or what will have transpired when the program has accomplished its objective.

Mrs. Crabtree, director of the WMU of Oak Grove Church, and her committee gathered their information and discussed what the church might do to minister to the migrant farm laborers and their families. They found that most of the adults could not read and write English. Some could not speak English. The children were at least two grade levels behind their respective ages. They also found that the families had very few changes of clothes. Most of the migrant workers claimed to be Catholic. Some had received Bibles and literature in Spanish at the Migrant Mission Center in Hope, Arkansas, but they had difficulty reading them.

Mrs. Crabtree's committee decided that the goal of their ministry would be to establish a mission to migrant farm laborers which would meet their basic spiritual, educational, and clothing needs. In order to accomplish this goal the church would provide regular worship and Bible study programs, teach them to read and write, bring the children up to grade, and teach the parents and older children to make some of their own clothes.

The third phase is *formulating specific objectives.* These should be stated as specific outcomes. Objectives break goals down into manageable steps. They serve as markers along the path to achieving the overall goals of a program.

Mrs. Crabtree's committee began to determine certain specific objectives that they would achieve as they established their mission. Objective 1 was to find a meeting place that would be close to the center of the housing for farm laborers. Since migrant farm laborers only stay for a short period of time, this objective had to be accomplished within a week. Objective 2 was to find literacy materials in both English and Spanish. This also had to be accomplished within a week.

Objective 3 was to find someone who had expertise in literacy training and in teaching English as a second language. This needed to be accomplished within two weeks. Objective 4 was to find schoolbooks that could be used to tutor the children. This needed to be done within two weeks. Objective 5 was to find persons who would donate their time to do the tutoring. Objective 6 was to find some cloth, portable sewing machines, and persons who knew how to cut out patterns and use the sewing machines.

Objective 7 was to firm up the agreement that the pastor and members of the choir would be prepared to implement the worship services on Saturdays (since this was the day off for the workers). Objective 8 was to find a piano and a pianist for the worship services. Objective 9 was to find Sunday School teachers to teach on Saturday, and to enlist them for the remainder of the harvest season. All of this had to be done within two weeks, or most of the harvest season would be over before they could begin.

3. Implementation Strategies

When the goals and objectives have been properly formulated, the implementation strategies are easy to develop. They are already resident in the objectives. First, the information about the client population and the program should be compiled and made available to the planning committee. The second step is scheduling the use of facilities. Third is the preparatory activity such as enlistment, orientation, training of workers, and gathering of resources, such as supplies and equipment. Fourth is preparing the budget and securing its approval by the appropriate sources. The fifth step is to develop procedures for allocating resources. These should be a part of the orientation and training materials. No program is going to be free of problems, and this is especially true if clearly stated procedures are not stipulated in advance. Sixth is development of instruments for monitoring and evaluating the program. These are generally record cards, record books, report forms, and an evaluation form. There should be a printed set of procedures for evaluation included in the workers' training. Program scheduling is the seventh strategy. This includes determining the length of time for each meeting and the starting and ending dates.

4. Implementation

Implementation means putting the strategies into practice. From the time the program begins, someone should be responsible for monitoring the process. Monitoring is an ongoing process of evaluation (some have called it "hip-pocket evaluation"). It makes use of the records, considers formal and informal personal interviews with both workers and clients, checks the use of supplies and other resources, and evaluates the relative effectiveness and efficiency of the program.

Periodic in-service training sessions need to be part of the implementation process. These sessions could also include periodic evaluations. Most workers (paid or volunteer) need to hear that they are doing a good job, and if they are not, they need help.

A checklist of things to do, times to start, and dates by which to have things done will help guide the social minister in the implementation of the program.

5. Evaluation

In addition to the regular monitoring process, periodic evaluations of the whole program should be made. Each objective should be studied. Three essential elements should guide the evaluation process: (1) *Effort*—How many hours, how much money, how many people, how much space, and what other resources went into the program? (2) *Effectiveness*—How well has the program functioned? Have the objectives been achieved? Is the program performing the service as expected? (3) *Efficiency*—Has the effectiveness been worth the effort? Have too many resources been used with little success? Could the same success be accomplished with less effort? Could the program be more effective if a different strategy or a different type of effort were employed? If a program is not doing all it can with the effort expended, it is not efficient, even if the objectives are being achieved. The goal of efficiency is quality service.[1]

6. Supervision

Every worker is responsible to someone. This fact is spelled out in the plans and implementation strategies. Workers should know who is responsible for giving direction to their work. Most of the time they can be expected to perform well without someone looking over their shoulder, but they need to know that there is someone to whom they can turn.

Seeing that workers do their jobs is *not* the primary goal of supervision. The primary goal is the delivery of the best possible service to the client. If both the supervisor and the supervisee keep this in mind, the work of each will be enhanced, and clients will benefit.

Supervision should take into account the level of instruction and the type of instruction given to the worker. This begins with an adequate job description that answers the following questions: Who performs what action? To accomplish what immediate result? With what tools, equipment, or work aids? Upon what instructions?[2]

Workers who have specific skills, experience, and/or education in an area should not be treated as beginners. The more sophistication workers have regarding their tasks, the more autonomy they should be given. Above all, the same Christian spirit, grounded in God's love and empowered by the Holy Spirit, should be directed toward workers and clients. It is inexcusable before God for workers to be treated as second-class citizens. They must be treated with respect as persons, not as things to be used.

Summary and Conclusions

Social ministry programs should be grounded in Christ, person-centered, need-oriented, well planned and supervised, and empowered by the Holy Spirit. Some programs should seek to enrich the lives of persons in the church and in the community as well. Others, perhaps most, should seek to prevent individuals, couples, families, and groups whose condition is that of well-being

---

[1]Tony Tripodi, Phillip Fellin, and Irwin Epstein, *Differential Social Program Evaluation* (Itasca, Ill.: F. E. Peacock Publishers, 1978), 38-45.

[2]Sidney Fine and Wretha Wiley, *An Introduction to Functional Job Analysis* (Kalamazoo: W. E. Upjohn Institute, 1971), 10-11.

from deteriorating into a state of dysfunction. Social ministry programs must continue to "throw out the lifeline" to persons in need of immediate help. Their condition may be mildly dysfunctional, acutely dysfunctional, or chronically dysfunctional. With appropriate dedication and commitment, Christians can find ways to help. That is what social ministry programs are all about. When social ministry programs are operated in this manner they will not only tell the good news of Jesus Christ; they will also be a living witness to Him.

Exercises for Review and Evaluation

1. Discuss the need to focus social ministry programs.
2. List and briefly describe four types of enrichment programs.
3. Briefly describe prevention programs.
4. Briefly describe treatment programs.
5. Outline the steps to ministry program planning.
6. Briefly discuss each of the six administrative guidelines for social ministry programs.